For Amy, Sam and Noah

All proceeds from *Quarantine Cocktails* to benefit

GIVING

KITCHEN

Giving Kitchen provides emergency assistance
to food service workers through financial support
and a network of community resources.

LEARN MORE

Pictures captured with the Apple iPhone Pro Max (11,12, 13) employing portrait mode
for post-production depth-of-field adjustments. And who doesn't love a little bokeh?

On the front cover is the Clover Club, recipe on page 23.
On the back, the Manhattan, recipe on page 16.

QUARANTINE

COCKTAILS

EST. 2020

Aviation Cocktail

2 oz. Junipero gin
¼ oz. Creme de Violette
¼ oz. maraschino liqueur
½ oz. lemon juice
Garnish: lemon twist,
Luxardo cherry

Place ingredients in
shaking tin, add ice, shake
for 15 seconds. Double
strain into a chilled coupe
glass, lower a Luxardo
cherry into bottom of
glass, express lemon twist
and discard.

Foreword

We all needed a distraction (or two) during the height of COVID-19's rampage across humanity. Eight weeks into quarantine here at home, with numerous Zoom happy hours to attend, I turned to our liquor cabinet to take stock.

My inventory consisted of several bottles of Hendrick's gin, a few of Kahlúa, and four different mostly empty tequila bottles, souvenirs of a trip Amy and I took to Mexico before we were married (we just celebrated 18 years). If I was going to make something more interesting than a basic margarita or gin & tonic, I needed to step up my game. I decided to buy the ingredients for a classic I'd enjoyed before, the *Aviation* cocktail (pictured at left). I had the Hendrick's but needed to track down bottles of Creme de Violette and Luxardo Maraschino liqueur. And so down the rabbit hole I went, posting a new cocktail on my Instagram account nearly daily for over a year. The result is in your hands!

The book wouldn't have been possible without the love and support of my family. Despite concerns from my mother-in-law that I was maybe enjoying this "research" a little too much, my brilliant and beautiful wife Amy was supportive of most of these shenanigans, including being my proofreader and editor. And that's no easy task! I hope that I've given our boys Sam and Noah a glimpse of the good stuff and that they retain a sophisticated palate well into the future.

If you are new to home mixology, check out *Getting Started* (page 6) and *The 12-ish Bottle Bar* (page 74) to get a sense of the gear and terminology used throughout the book.

Proceeds from this book will be donated to *Giving Kitchen*, an Atlanta-based charity that provides emergency assistance to food service workers through financial support and a network of resources. Their community was hard-hit by COVID-19, and this is my way of giving back.

I hope you enjoy these cocktails as much as I did learning, making, and drinking them. *L'chaim*!

- Joey Trotz, November 2021
Instagram: @jetrotz

Table of Contents

Hemingway Daiquiri, pg. 39

Getting Started

If you already know what you're doing, feel free to skip past this section. But even seasoned home mixologists will hopefully find helpful tidbits here that I've learned and tested throughout the 18+ months I've spent creating these drinks. In addition to this introductory section, you'll find tips & tricks boxes scattered throughout the volume, although I'll cover the most important concepts here.

The sheer variety of liquors can be overwhelming, but you can make pretty much everything in this book with a modest investment in your home bar inventory. Check out *The 12(ish) Bottle Bar* guide on page 74 for my recommendations.

Glassware

Look - a Solo cup will hold your cocktail just fine, but there's no denying that a beautiful glass elevates that old mixology magic.

You can get away with just a few different glasses to start your adventure. But over time, finding new and cool glassware can be rather addictive.

The old-fashioned glass, also known as the double old-fashioned, the DOF, the rocks glass, or even just a plain-old tumbler, is a key part of your glassware collection. Obviously, you'll use this for all manner of drinks served on the rocks like the eponymous *Old-fashioned*, as well as some drinks served neat like the *Sazerac*. If you don't have any tiki mugs, a tumbler is an acceptable stand-in for serving many tropical drinks over crushed ice, as well as your classic margarita.

The coupe is the next critical cocktail glass. Initially used exclusively to serve Champagne, the coupe (and its close cousin, the Nick & Nora) is the go-to vessel for pretty much any cocktail strained and served without ice.

While some rumors (incorrectly) suggest the coupe was modeled after Marie Antoinette's breast, the design does serve a particular function.[1] The extra volume provided by the wide shape of the glass creates more surface area for the bubbly to be exposed to air. In turn, the Champagne can interact with more oxygen, allowing flavors and aromas to develop over time.

The voluminous V-shaped martini glass of the 1980s overshadowed the coupe for a while, but as the cocktail renaissance of the early 2000s took hold, the coupe became the go-to glassware and remains so today. Who needs to drink an eight-ounce martini anyway?

For so-called long drinks, meaning cocktails of higher volume typically "lengthened" by mixers like tonic or soda, we turn to the collins glass. A pint glass or other tall but ideally narrow glass can substitute. In a pinch, these can also be used for tiki drinks poured over fresh ice. A footed pilsner glass is my choice for drinks like the *Improved Chartreuse Swizzle*.

If you want to go overboard, there are even glasses made for specific drinks. The *Fogg Cutter* sports its own namesake glass, and the *Hurricane* uses, well - a hurricane glass. Tiki mugs are an increasingly sensitive topic given issues of cultural appropriation. So I personally have a couple of hand-thrown earthenware mugs, a skull (from Savannah's *Pirates House* restaurant), and a bright yellow parrot.

Measurement

Like baking, it pays to be precise with your cocktails. Otherwise, results will be inconsistent and difficult to troubleshoot. So leave the free-pouring styling of Tom Cruise and the (awful) movie *Cocktail* to the silver screen. The balance between sweet, sour, and alcohol are the name of the game here. If you are off by a ¼ ounce, the drink will just not be what it should be. Feel free to experiment - but start with a known set of specs to inform later variations.

I keep two jiggers on hand. One is a squat 2-ounce mini-measuring cup, and the other is a tall two-sided Japanese jigger. I use an OXO 2-ounce mini measuring cup with clear marks for ounces, teaspoons, and milliliters. It's also large enough to squeeze your citrus into without spilling everywhere. The Japanese jigger allows for very precise measurements. Less surface area in the tall format makes for an improved margin of error.

For many purposes, from stirring to ladling ingredients measured by the bar spoon, you'll need a bar spoon, 'natch. Ideally, you'll want a twisted handle (helpful for twirling while stirring) with a weighted flat end for quick muddling or ice cracking duty.

I don't expect you to measure your dashes or bar spoons in milliliters (it's 3.697 ml to the bar spoon),

> ## "Think like a scientist and you will make better drinks."
> ## — Dave Arnold
> ## *Liquid Intelligence*

but there are a few guidelines. A recipe calling for a dash refers to one hard downward shake of a standard-sized bitters bottle and two shakes if you use a Japanese bitters bottle. And the bar spoon is ¾ teaspoons if you want to get really accurate!

Ingredients added at low volumes are inevitably the most potent flavors and the ones we will mess up first. So the time-honored tradition is to build a drink from cheapest components to most expensive. Begin with citrus, bitters, syrups, etc., then add your expensive booze last. This way, you are less likely to throw out your priciest liquor. Of course, feel free to drink your mistakes and chalk them up as a learning experience. And one other rule - don't build your drink in the mixing glass or shaker over ice. Liquor will immediately begin to melt your ice, diluting your precious drink. Add ice and shake or stir only once everything is set - and that includes your prepared garnishes and chilled glassware.

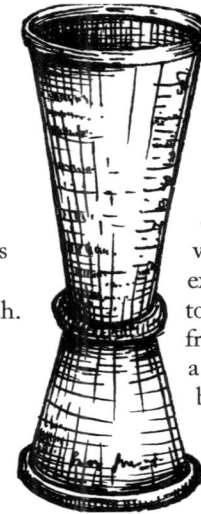

Mixing & Shaking

Shaken or stirred - that is the question. And despite James Bond's advice to the contrary, we don't shake all-spirit drinks like martinis. If a cocktail includes fruit juice, we shake to chill and aerate, dilute, and add texture to the final product. Those are not attributes we want in most all-liquor drinks.

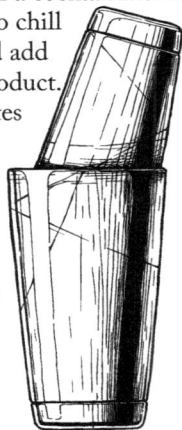

For shaken cocktails, you'll need a good shaking tin. A mason jar is excellent in a pinch, and you can even find perforated lids to make pouring easier. But if you plan to make many cocktails at home, I'd recommend a pair of so-called Boston shaker tins. These are two food-quality aluminum vessels, one slightly larger than the other, often weighted at the bottom for better balance. I collected a few cobbler shakers over the years but got rid of them as I delved into this hobby. Cobbler shakers, a tin with a cap and a strainer built-in, have a tendency to freeze shut, trapping our precious cocktail inside. Trust me - stick with the Boston tins!

Shaking technique is among the most arcane areas of mixology. A decade ago, there were endless arguments about different methods, ranging from your typical up/down or side-to-side to the frenetic multi-directional approach pioneered by Japanese bartenders. So while it may look cool, it's really unnecessary.

Regardless of how you shake, as long as you do it for about 15 seconds, your drink is going to be diluted appropriately and well-chilled. Any longer will introduce too much water, and any shorter won't provide the chill or texture you are looking for.

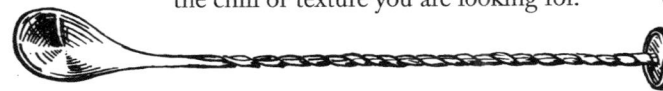

For shaken drinks, I've adopted Dave Arnold's scientifically proven technique of using one large 2-inch piece of ice (ideally clear, see *Water & Ice*, page 9) and two smaller cubes from the typical freezer's ice maker. Combining a sizeable chilling surface with small ice to melt and dilute the drink works well in most applications. The large cube will barely melt during the shaking but has the volume to introduce a ton of bubbles and texture into the drink. The smaller cubes will almost melt away to nothing and drive most of the dilution

we're looking for. If you don't have large-format ice, just use a whole tin of ice fresh from the freezer.

We use the whip shake for quite a few of these cocktails (no, I'm not referring to Devo). Primarily used for tiki drinks served over crushed or pebble ice, a whip shake is used when minimal dilution is desired, as the drink will dilute over time. In this technique, we add a half-handful or about an ounce of crushed ice to our tin and shake until we don't hear the ice knocking about in the shaker.

Lastly, there's the dry shake. Used to emulsify drinks with egg white, shake with no ice in the tin to create the desired texture before adding ice for a second round of shaking to chill and dilute the cocktail.

Stirring

Stirring is the mixing technique for spirit-only cocktails. While a mixing tin or a pint glass will work, ideally, you'll want a nice heavy-bottomed mixing glass. Some of these are just beautiful and look great sitting on your bar cart. See *Resources*, page 72.

With a spirit-forward drink, we want it smooth and ice-cold. Despite a lack of scientific evidence, shaking is often thought to "bruise" a spirit by suppressing the subtle oak of aged spirits and the botanical flavors of herbaceous gins. Without fresh juice, eggs, or dairy to provide structure, our goal is to keep a silky-smooth texture.

I'll readily admit to being no master in the art of stirring. There's a trick to pushing the bar spoon back and forth with your lower fingers while the top of the spoon rotates in the pocket between your thumb and pointer finger. Easier said than done, but having a bar spoon with a twisted shaft will help. Try to focus on keeping the back of the spoon against the glass. That way, the spoon will naturally turn in the direction of your stirring as you push/pull with your fingers. A rule of thumb is that 40 revolutions will give desired chilling and dilution. If you have room, keep your mixing glass in the freezer for even more effective chilling.

Straining

Next in your arsenal will be a strainer (or three). You will need what's called a Hawthorne strainer (left) that fits inside your shaking tins or mixing glass to hold back the ice and other unsavory elements you don't want in your cocktail glass. You will also need a small fine-mesh strainer (2 inches or so) for double straining when you want to avoid ice crystals ruining the texture created by your fabulous shaking technique. Lastly, if you make many stirred drinks, a Julep strainer (right) will be an elegant addition to your bar kit.

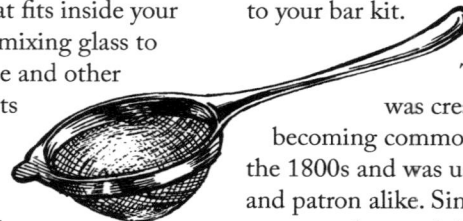

The julep strainer was created just as ice was becoming commonly available in the 1800s and was used by bartender and patron alike. Since straws were not commonplace and dental hygiene wasn't what it is today, drinkers would protect sensitive teeth by using their own personal julep strainer to hold back the ice.

Citrus, Muddling & Other Prep

If you follow my adventure into home bartending, you'll soon find a good portion of your refrigerator devoted to a variety of citrus. To keep mine organized and fresh, I store lemons and limes in zip-top bags, as well as a few oranges and grapefruit.

A good quality Y-shaped peeler (left) is required for twists, zests, and peeling in general. I prefer a rubberized version from OXO. Be careful - these can cut you quite easily.

All that citrus means we need a good hand-juicer (right). Avoid those with enamel - the coating will flake off eventually, and that's not what we want in our cocktails! I keep two types, a smaller squeeze-type version for limes and lemons (left) and a larger reamer for oranges and grapefruit.

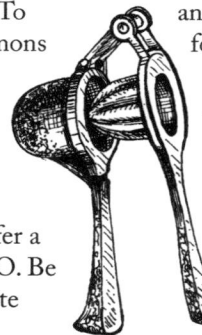

A muddler (right) is essential for a slew of drinks. While you can make do with the previously mentioned weighted bar spoon, you will want to pick up a nice solid wooden or plastic muddler (no teeth, please). This will let you gently release oils from herbs and juice from fruit, all without pulverizing your ingredients to such a degree that they end up in your guests' teeth or stuck in a straw.

Water & Ice

One unwritten ingredient in every cocktail is water, most often provided by melted ice. Ice not only chills a drink but contributes 25% or more to its volume. So let's talk about this crucial component.

Ice really kick-started the cocktail as we know it. Before the mid-1800s, ice was not widely available, but later in the century, the ice trade exploded, with ice traveling all the way to tropical climates. How could ice be stored on hot sailing ships for months at a time? Well, it all boils down to physics, and those physics inform how we use ice in mixing cocktails.

To wax scientific for a moment, ice melts in a given period proportional to how much heat is transferred into the ice and its exposed surface area. The larger the ice block, the slower it melts. Long before the invention of commercial refrigeration, blocks of ice, five feet or larger, were shipped from the Arctic. Huge buildings known as ice houses could store the frozen goodness, even in tropical climates, for months on end.

Clear ice has a lot of advantages - it's beautiful in the glass, it melts more slowly, and due to fewer impurities, it shatters less easily, allowing for greater control over dilution. So while you don't have to use clear ice, it's certainly an elegant addition to your home bar repertoire. I love my clear-ice freezer by *Epare*, pictured left (see *Resources* page 72).

Clear ice is created by directional freezing, typically top-to-bottom. Picture an open-topped cooler, insulating the sides but not the top. By preventing cold from entering the sides or bottom and only from above, bubbles and impurities are pushed down as the ice freezes, leaving crystal-clear ice on top and a layer of cloudy ice below.

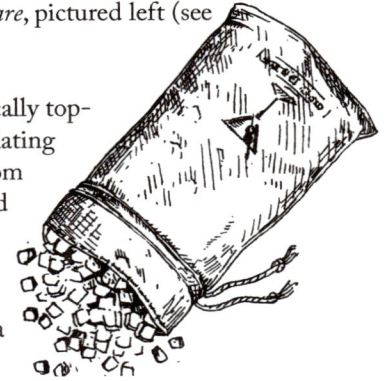

Another tool I love is what's called a Lewis Bag (pictured above). Originally used by banks to transport coins, crafty 19th-century bartenders co-opted it for drink preparation, taking advantage of the canvas sack's durability and ability to absorb excess water.

For any drinks that call for crushed or cracked ice, the Lewis Bag and accompanying wooden mallet can create the most perfectly snowy ice you can imagine. While I'd love to pick up a pebble ice-maker for the house, I make do with a couple of Target's house brand Houdini pebble ice trays (pictured at right) for my tiki concoctions. Now, let's make some drinks!

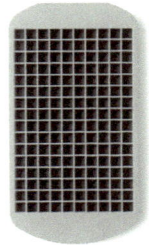

Chapter One:
All about that barrel-aged goodness

The most popular spirit in classic cocktails is whisk(e)y, regardless of how you prefer to spell it. The archetypal example is the Old-fashioned, "old" because barkeeps of yore would fancy up a base combination of whiskey, sugar, and bitters with liqueurs or similar "enhancements." As a result, the boomers of the time would ask for their drink "the old-fashioned way."

The word "whiskey" comes from the Latin for distilled spirits or *aqua vitae*, the water of life. In Scotland and Ireland, this became *uisge beatha*, eventually anglicized and shortened to *uisge*, and finally, *whiskey*. Babylonians and Greeks were known to create distilled spirits, which ultimately entered Europe through monasteries and early practitioners of secular medicine. By the 15th century, consumption was at least in part recreational.

While the first known literary reference to whiskey distillation comes from Chaucer's *Canterbury Tales* in the 1500s,[2] American whiskey is the product of English, Irish, and Scottish immigrants hundreds of years later. In the mid-Atlantic British colonies, tobacco was the cash crop of choice, and rye was often planted to replenish nutrients in the soil. As the American Revolution soured colonists on drinking English rum, they turned their attention closer to home where (in the Northern states) rye was plentiful, and farms began distilling their surplus grain. When the fledgling government began collecting an excise tax, "The Whiskey Rebellion" broke out. Some

farmers in western Pennsylvania packed up shop and moved south to Kentucky, where government taxation was lax, and corn, not rye, was the common grain. And soon after, American bourbon was born.[3]

I've concentrated here primarily on whiskey cocktails of the 19th and 20th centuries using bourbon and rye. Like European wines, the early colonial distillers turned to barrel-aging to bring character to these spirits. Barrels are porous, expanding and contracting over time, and drive three critical processes: evaporation, oxidation, and extraction.

Whiskey Sour

In evaporation, the liquid lost to the atmosphere (sometimes called "The Angel's Share") concentrates the spirit's flavors. Oxidation is the reverse - oxygen enters the barrel through the wood, infusing notes of oak esters into the liquid. Extraction is the chemical interaction between the fluid and the wood itself, bringing other flavorful compounds like vanillin and tannin to the party.[4]

That's a lot of complexity developed in the barrel and captured in the bottle, so while I enjoy the world of whiskey cocktails, I also covet the fantastic flavors in whiskey sipped neat – there's a lot to appreciate.

The Old-Fashioned

Ingredients

2 oz. rye or bourbon whiskey
1 bar spoon simple syrup
1 dash Angostura bitters
1 dash Regans orange bitters
Garnish: 1 wide swath of both lemon and orange peel, plus as many good cherries as you'd like!

Directions

In a chilled mixing glass, combine ingredients. Fill mixing glass with cracked ice and stir until outside of glass is frosty and the drink is diluted to taste, around 30-40 seconds. Strain into an old-fashioned glass over a two-inch rock of ice.

Cut a swath of peel, including a reasonably thick bit of white pith, hold about one inch over glass, then pinch to express oils. Nestle peels between glass wall and ice cube. Garnish with cherries on a pick.

MIXOLOGY TIP: CLEAR ICE

Get yourself a large-format silicone ice mold. These come in a variety of shapes, including squares and spheres. If you're feeling fancy, get a clear-ice mold for the most beautiful drinks imaginable. See *Water & Ice*, page 9 and *Resources*, page 72.

The Old-fashioned

Bloom County

This complex bourbon cocktail comes from one of my favorite YouTube cocktail experts, *The Educated Barfly*.[7] And while some of the ingredients are relatively obscure, all will find a home in many a tropical cocktail. The first of these is allspice dram, a potent Caribbean pimento-based liqueur. The other is Licor 43, a vanilla-forward Spanish spirit based on an ancient and closely guarded secret recipe.[8]

2 oz. bourbon whiskey, 100-proof
½ oz. Licor 43 liqueur
½ oz. Amaro Montenegro
2 dashes Peychaud's bitters
⅛ oz. St. Elizabeth's allspice dram
Garnish: orange twist

Combine all ingredients in your cocktail shaker and shake for 15 seconds until well diluted. Double strain into a chilled coupe glass. Express twist and garnish.

Algonquin

This is the namesake drink of the Algonquin Hotel - my home away from home when travel was still a thing, and I was working out of *The Weather Company's* New York City office. This cocktail was great after a long day of meetings, especially when Hamlet, the hotel's resident cat, would make an appearance in the lobby. The tradition of a resident hotel cat began in the 1920s when Dorothy Parker held court at the hotel leading the famous Round Table.[6] I made this in late Spring 2020, as I wasn't expecting to visit again anytime soon.

1½ oz. rye whiskey
¾ oz. Dolin blanc or
¾ oz. Dolin dry vermouth (for a drier cocktail)
½ oz. pineapple gomme syrup or
½ oz. pineapple juice (for a drier cocktail)

Combine ingredients and shake for 15 seconds until well diluted. Double strain into a chilled coupe glass.

Amaro Mood

This is a great place to begin if you want to explore the bittersweet notes of the wide range of spirits known as amari. I've fallen in love with the grappa-based Amaro Nonino Quintessentia - a perfect introduction to the genre. This cocktail combines a backbone of bourbon balanced with Nonino and another amaro - the artichoke-based Cynar - making for a complex drink perfect for sipping.[5]

1½ oz. bourbon
¾ oz. Amaro Nonino
¾ oz. Cynar
4 dashes Angostura bitters
Garnish: orange twist

Combine all ingredients in mixing glass, add ice, and stir well until well-chilled and diluted. Strain into a rocks glass over a large cube. Express orange, rub rim, drop into drink.

Amaretto Sour, Improved

This is an adaptation that comes by way of bartender Jeffrey Morgenthaler, author of *The Bar Book*, one of my favorites. To improve on what was often an unbalanced and overly sweet drink from the 1970s, he adds high-proof bourbon to offset that sweetness and deliver more punch. [9]

Ingredients

1½ oz. barrel-strength bourbon
¾ oz. Amaretto Disaronno
1 oz. lemon juice
½ oz. egg white or aquafaba
1 tsp. rich simple syrup (2:1, see page 68)
Garnish: lemon twist and cherries

Directions

Combine all ingredients in your cocktail shaker. Close the shaker and use the dry shake technique (shaken without ice) for 30 seconds to emulsify. When you dry shake, there's no ice to make the tins contract from the cold and lock together, so be careful if you don't want to end up wearing your cocktail. After the dry shake, fill the tin with ice and shake for 15 seconds until well-chilled and diluted. Pour over a big rock in an old-fashioned glass. Garnish with a lemon twist and a few high-quality cherries (see tip below).

MIXOLOGY TIP!
Do yourself a favor and skip the neon-red "maraschino" cherries you see in most markets. Luxardo and Amarenas can usually be found on Amazon, or at your local specialty market.

The Last…Cocktail Ratio?

The *Last Word* is far from the final statement on 4-ingredient cocktails, but it could be one of my favorites. Originally the Prohibition-era signature drink of the *Detroit Athletic Club*, the recipe was published in the 1950s but didn't become part of the cocktail revolution until just this side of the turn of the century. It was almost lost to obscurity until it was rescued in the mid-aughts by a Seattle bartender.[10]

It's incredible how different the variations taste, with considerable swings in flavor profile but barely adjusted components. The possibilities here are endless and serve as a great template for further experimentation.

One variant, the *Paper Plane* (page 17), made up of equal parts bourbon, Amaro Nonino Quintessentia, and lemon, is one of my absolute favorites. See other variant ideas below.

If nothing else, the *Last Word* and the *Final Ward* are exhibits 1 and 2 in the case of *Why You Should Buy a Bottle of Green Chartreuse.* See my bottle recommendations, page 74.

Equal Parts Cocktail Variants[11]

- Pete's Word: Laphroaig 10-year, lime, maraschino, green Chartreuse
- Lumiere: gin, lemon, St-Germain, green Chartreuse
- Naked and Famous: mezcal, lime, Aperol, yellow Chartreuse
- Dirty Word: tequila, lime, maraschino, green Chartreuse
- Third Ward: tequila, grapefruit, maraschino, yellow Chartreuse
- Right Word: gin, lime, St-Germain, Lillet blanc
- Industry Sour: Fernet Branca, lime, simple syrup, green Chartreuse
- Bad Word: gin, lime, Gran Classico, green Chartreuse
- That's My Word: gin, lime, St-Germain, yellow Chartreuse
- Penultimate Word: bourbon, lemon, peach liqueur, Averna
- Half Hour Flight: bourbon, lemon, Aperol, Ancho Reyes chili liqueur
- Latest Word: genever, lime, Maraschino, green Chartreuse
- Shaddock: genever, lemon, St-Germain, Aperol
- La Ultima Palabra: mezcal, lime, maraschino liqueur, green Chartreuse
- Eulogy: batavia arrack, lime, velvet falernum, yellow Chartreuse

14

Last Word (left) and Final Ward (right)

Last Word

Ingredients

¾ oz. London dry gin
¾ oz. green Chartreuse
¾ oz. maraschino liqueur
¾ oz. lime juice
Garnish: lime twist

Directions

Combine all ingredients, then fill your shaker with ice and shake until chilled and diluted, about 15 seconds. Double strain into a chilled coupe. Garnish.

Final Ward

Ingredients

¾ oz. rye
¾ oz. green Chartreuse
¾ oz. maraschino liqueur
¾ oz. lemon juice
Garnish: lemon twist

Directions

Combine all ingredients, then fill your shaker with ice and shake until chilled and diluted, about 15 seconds. Double strain into a chilled coupe. Garnish. [12]

Monte Cassino

This equal parts cocktail is also modeled on the *Last Word*, but uses yellow Chartreuse, green's sweeter and mellower cousin. Yellow comes in at 80-proof, versus green's sharper 110. Green also tends to be slightly drier than the yellow version. A spicy barrel-proof Rittenhouse rye is ideal here, holding up well against both liqueurs. Created in the 1500s, Bénédictine is infused with 27 plants and spices, bringing plenty of complexity to the glass.[13]

Ingredients

¾ oz. Rittenhouse rye
¾ oz. yellow Chartreuse
¾ oz. Bénédictine
¾ oz. lemon juice

Directions

Combine all ingredients, then fill your shaker with ice and shake until chilled and diluted, about 15 seconds. Double strain into a chilled coupe, then express a lemon twist over and garnish.

Monte Cassino

KNOW YOUR LIQUEURS

Chartreuse is a wonderful French liqueur made by Carthusian Monks with a sweet, spicy, and distinctly herbal profile. Tasting notes include mint, sage, gentian, apple, and vanilla. Its complex character would have helped mask the poor quality of bathtub gin during Prohibition.

The Manhattan

Sweet

Boozy

Spicy

The classics are among the best places to start your cocktail journey, and the widely available ingredients in the *Manhattan* make for a satisfying sipper. Start with the traditional recipe below, then experiment. You could swap bourbon for rye or vary the proportions, although the 2:1:2 is the classic.

Ingredients

2 oz. rye or bourbon
1 oz. Carpano Antica Formula sweet red vermouth
  or
1 oz. Cocchi di Torino sweet red vermouth
2 dashes Angostura bitters
Optional: 1 bar spoon Luxardo cherry syrup
Garnish: Luxardo cherries

Directions

Add all ingredients to mixing glass. Add ice and stir for 30-40 seconds, or until well-diluted (see tip below). Double strain either up in a chilled coupe or over a large rock in an old-fashioned glass. Garnish with as many cherries as you'd like!

DILUTION CHECK

Keep a metal straw with your mixology kit. When mixing drinks, dip the tip into your mixture, put your finger on the opening and pull out a straw-sized taste to confirm it's good to go!

Paper Plane

Oh boy is this one a revelation - and possibly my favorite cocktail of all time. This is a bona fide gateway drug to introduce anyone to bourbon and amaro. It's an equal-parts cocktail, essentially a riff on the *Last Word* (see page 15). It features Amaro Nonino Quintessentia, an Italian amaro with a grappa base, and notes of botanicals, alpine herbs, and orange peel. In a pinch, Amaro Montenegro is a good substitute.

Although the drink seems like it came out of the heyday of pre-Prohibition bar culture, it was actually invented in 2008 by award-winning bartender Sam Ross (who also created the *Penicillin*, see page 69). The drink first appeared on the opening menu of *The Violet Hour* in Chicago, a bar where Ross was consulting. It was so popular in Chicago that he brought it back to his bar *Milk & Honey* in New York City and the rest is history.

The M.I.A. hit *Paper Plane* was the inspiration for the name, and the drink was garnished with a tiny paper airplane. Ross recommends a higher-proof bourbon and warns not to overshake the drink; it's easy to over dilute.[14]

You can also try substituting grapefruit juice for lemon to make *Esprit d'Escalier* or replace bourbon with tequila for the *Avion de Papel*.

Ingredients

¾ oz. barrel-proof bourbon
¾ oz. Aperol
¾ oz. Amaro Nonino Quintessentia
¾ oz. lemon juice
Garnish: tiny paper plane

Directions

Add all ingredients to shaker. Add ice and shake for about 15 seconds. Double strain into a chilled coupe. Garnish with a lemon slice or twist.

FRESH SQUEEZED

The difference between fresh-squeezed citrus and the bottled stuff is truly night and day. The cocktail wonks say that even a few hours is enough to reduce quality dramatically. So squeeze those lemons and limes *à la minute*.

Fulton County

Named for the county where I live, I created this peach *Manhattan* variant to celebrate Atlanta's historic impact on the 2020 election. To go all-out Georgia, use Atlanta-based distilleries ASW Resurgens Rye and Blended Family's peach liqueur.

Ingredients

Sweet
———
Boozy

2 oz. rye whiskey
¼ oz. peach syrup
  or
¼ oz. peach liqueur
¾ oz. Dolin Dry white vermouth
1 dash Fee Brothers peach bitters
1 dash Fee Brothers barrel-aged aromatic bitters
Garnish: peach slice

Directions

Add all ingredients except garnish to a mixing glass. Fill with ice and stir for 30-40 seconds until well-chilled and diluted. Strain into a chilled coupe. Garnish with a thin peach slice.

STORING VERMOUTH

If you think you don't like vermouth in your martini, you've probably been doing it wrong. Store your vermouth in the refrigerator, where it will keep for a few months. Room temperature does this spirit no favors. Try the *Repour* oxidation-reducing stoppers to prolong shelf life. See *Resources*, page 72.

Surf Liner

Who knew whiskey could go tiki? This drink follows a common tiki theme, using an almond syrup known as orgeat (see recipe, page 70). We use the whip shake method here, shaking with a small amount of crushed ice, an ideal technique for strong drinks served over crushed ice to minimize dilution.[16]

2 oz. rye whiskey
1 oz. pineapple juice
¾ oz. fresh lemon juice
¾ oz. orgeat
¾ oz. pineapple syrup
2 dashes Peychaud's bitters

Combine all the ingredients in a shaker. Whip shake until the sound of the ice in your shaker is gone. Strain over crushed ice in a double old-fashioned glass.

American Negroni

Created in Italy out of a tradition of bitter aperitifs meant for sipping before dinner, the *Negroni* cocktail (more versions on pages 34-35) typically uses gin as the base spirit. Here, we swap in bourbon to significant effect.[15]

1¼ oz. bourbon
1 oz. Cocchi di Torino or Carpano Antica
¾ oz. Aperol
¾ oz. Campari
1 dash Angostura bitters
Garnish: lemon twist and cherries

Add all ingredients to mixing glass. Fill glass with ice. Stir for 30-40 seconds until well-diluted. Serve over a big rock in an old-fashioned glass, express twist over glass and garnish with cherries on a pick.

Dale's Julep

This is a variation on the classic *Mint Julep*, created by the famous bartender Dale Degroff.[17] It suits my Georgia-born roots.

2 oz. barrel-proof bourbon
½ oz. Blended Family peach liqueur
2 slices peach
10 sprigs mint
Garnish: more mint and another peach slice

In your mixing glass, combine mint with the peach and liqueur. Gently muddle - we don't want to shred the herbs, just bruise them. Add the bourbon and stir. Strain into a metal julep cup. Add crushed ice while stirring, working slowly, incorporating the ingredients. Continue packing cup with crushed ice until it forms a mound atop the drink. Garnish with a good bunch of mint, peach slice and insert straw.

19

Congregational Cocktails

Purim is a holiday that tells the story of a time the Jewish people escaped extermination. The villain of that story is Haman and the heroes are the Jewish leader Mordechai and his cousin, Queen Esther. There is a Talmudic tradition that makes drunkenness during Purim a mitzvah (good deed). We fulfill the mitzvah when we've imbibed enough - *shikkered*, as my dad (ז״ל) would have said in Yiddish - and can't tell the difference between the good guys and bad.

I'm happy to call Congregation Shearith Israel my family's spiritual home and am thankful for my synagogue's leadership during the pandemic. When we could not gather in 2021 as a community for our annual Purim celebration (and the drinking that ensues), we sent home hospitality bags to every family. The gift bags featured the lovely glassware seen at right, as well as the recipe card designed by congregant Jamie Wender, featuring several of my Judaic cocktails.

The King's Ring

The wine float here atop a modified *Whiskey Sour* is meant to recall the moment in the Megillah when the king offers up his ring to Haman.[18]

Ingredients

2 oz. rye or bourbon
1 oz. lemon juice
¾ oz. simple syrup
1 oz. egg white or aquafaba
½ oz. red wine

Directions

Combine all but the red wine in shaker. Dry shake (without ice) for 30 seconds to emulsify, then again with ice. Double strain over a big rock. Position a spoon at the top of the foam near the center of the glass, slowly pour wine over the back of spoon.

The King's Ring

Maror Tai

I created this interpretation of the *Artichoke Hold* (page 43) for Passover 2020. It's a bitter reminder of our servitude in ancient Egypt and packs a punch to boot.

¾ oz. Smith & Cross overproof rum
¾ oz. Cynar
¾ oz. Campari
½ oz. St-Germain
¾ oz. lime juice
½ oz. orgeat
¼ tsp. grated white horseradish
Garnish: bitter herb, Angostura bitters

Add all ingredients to shaker. Add ice, shake about 15 seconds. Double strain over fresh crushed ice in a double old-fashioned glass. Add bitters and grate horseradish over the top.

The Whole Megillah

Here's a mocktail to satisfy not only the kids but the non-drinking adults among us. This one has it all. In other words, it's "the whole megillah!" The drink's name refers to the practice of reading the story of Purim - you guessed it - the Megillah - in one sitting. We've got multiple juices, a touch of sugar, plus a bit of delicious vanilla thrown in too!

1 oz. pineapple juice
1 oz. orange juice
½ oz. lime juice
¾ oz. orgeat, or simple syrup
4 drops vanilla extract
Sprig of mint

Shake like crazy with just a little ice, then strain into an old-fashioned glass with fresh ice. For an optional garnish, you can drop in the spent lime shell you squeezed for the juice along with a lightly bruised sprig of mint.

Hamantaschen

This drink's name comes from a classic baked Purim treat that recalls the tricornered hat worn by Haman. A hamantaschen is a jelly-filled pastry, and here we use sweet jelly and fresh fruit to bring balance to this gin sour. Inspired by Sasha Petraske's *Cosmonaut*.[19]

2 oz. London dry gin
¾ oz. lemon juice
1 tsp. berry preserves
7 fresh berries
1 hamantaschen

Combine the gin, lemon juice, preserves and four of the berries in your shaker. Fill with ice and shake vigorously until frosty. Strain into an old-fashioned glass over fresh ice. Garnish with the additional berries. Enjoy a hamantaschen chaser on the side!

Chapter Two:
We're not talking bathtubs here

Martinis, brambles, and tonics, oh my!

Gin, like all spirits, starts as a colorless, odorless, and flavorless distillate. When those genius Dutch developed an approach hundreds of years ago to infuse botanicals into clear spirits, gin was born.

Genever is the original gin, dating back to 16th-century Holland. The base grains are malted, similar to whiskey, giving it a robust flavor. It's also infused with juniper and botanicals, but less so than other later styles. Different gins steep fresh or dried citrus peels before distillation, driving a bright, citrus flavor - and why a twist of lemon really performs magic in a martini.

London Dry Gin, the most well-known, is defined as gin infused with botanical flavor through re-distillation with no added sugars. Despite the name, it does not have to be made in London, but its prominent flavor must come from juniper. Other spices often used include cardamom, spruce or various roots. You name it, there's probably a gin that has it.

Plymouth Gin, however, is made only in Plymouth, England. Slightly sweeter with a more oily texture than London dry, it tastes earthier with less juniper.

New World or American Gin has become a thing of late, with celebrity gins like *Deadpool's* (aka Ryan Reynolds) Aviation Gin competing with brands like Bluecoat and Anchor Junipero. Aviation Gin is often noted to have flavors of sassafras or birch, while others have more cardamom or herbal notes. I enjoy Junipero - it's a true juniper flavor-bomb, perfect when you want a punchy profile for your gin cocktail.[20]

Now is as good a time as any to note that there is nary a vodka cocktail in this volume. Why, you ask? To me, vodka is a one-trick pony. Distilled alcohol with no other additions is just - distilled alcohol. By definition, vodka possesses little flavor and almost no nuance. But gin? The possibilities are endless.

Lillet Martini

Ingredients

2 oz. Plymouth gin
1 oz. Lillet Blanc
1 dash Regans orange bitters
Garnish: see below

Directions

In a chilled mixing glass, combine ingredients. Fill mixing glass with cracked ice and stir until outside of glass is frosty and the drink is diluted to taste, 30 to 40 seconds. Strain into an ice cold coupe and garnish with the ingredient of your choice - lemon, onion, or olive.

The Clover Club

The *Clover Club* cocktail dates back to the late 1800s and Philadelphia's Bellevue-Stratford Hotel.

It emerged from a Philadelphia men's group called (you guessed it) the Clover Club that met regularly at the Bellevue-Stratford Hotel from the 1880s to the 1920s. The *Clover Club* cocktail was likely concocted around the turn of the century and at first exclusively imbibed by club members. When the hotelier of the Bellevue-Stratford moved to the Waldorf Astoria Hotel, the drink made its way to New York City.[21]

This was my first-ever attempt at using fresh egg white in a cocktail. I chickened out (pun intended) and used pasteurized egg white, which works just fine. The impact can't be beaten - texture, mouthfeel, and beautiful color gradations all stem from that shaken egg white. A little aquafaba (the liquid from canned chickpeas) is an excellent alternative.

For this cocktail, I also made a fruit syrup for the first time (see recipe on page 70). Julie Reiner of NYC's *Clover Club* updated the eponymous classic with ½ ounce of dry white vermouth for a more balanced flavor profile.[22]

Ingredients

1½ oz. Plymouth gin
½ oz. fresh lemon juice
½ oz. Dolin dry vermouth
½ oz. raspberry syrup
¼ oz. egg white or aquafaba

Directions

Add all ingredients to tin and dry shake for 30 seconds to emulsify. Open tins and fill with ice. Shake for another 15 seconds until frosty. Double strain into a chilled coupe. No garnish necessary, but a raspberry wouldn't hurt!

Bonus Tip: Swap the simple syrup with St-Germain elderflower liqueur for a more floral cocktail.

Corpse Reviver No. 2

The Corpse Reviver No. 2 belongs to a family of pre-Prohibition cocktails able to "rouse the drinker from the dead." In other words, every bar had its version of a "reviver" drink, all meant to cure hangovers, increase vigor and otherwise improve one's morning.[23]

This version comes from the classic *Savoy Cocktail Book* (1930),[24] which claimed that four of these taken in quick succession would reanimate the dead. I'll have to get back to you on that, but in the meantime, enjoy. I used Herbsaint, the New Orleans anise-flavored liqueur, in this drink the first time I made it as I had a tough time tracking down a bottle of absinthe. I use an inexpensive food-grade atomizer to mist the inside of the glass instead of rinsing - less waste, more taste! The scent of anise here teases the senses as you sip from the glass. Heavenly.

Ingredients

Absinthe or Herbsaint, to rinse (see note below)
¾ oz. London dry gin
¾ oz. Lillet Blanc
¾ oz. Cointreau
¾ oz. lemon juice, freshly squeezed

Directions

Combine all ingredients in your shaking tin. Fill with ice and shake for 15 seconds. Double strain into a chilled coupe.

Know your spirits: Absinthe

Absinthe is an anise-flavored high-proof spirit with many botanicals, including its namesake *artemisia absinthium* (grand wormwood). The spirit often has a pale green color and earned the nickname "*la fée verte*" (the green fairy). It was much beloved by figures of the bohemian movement of the late 19th century and was a key ingredient in New Orleans' famous *Sazerac* cocktail. Absinthe was banned across the U.S. in 1912 because of perceived psychoactive aspects and wasn't legalized until 2007 after being proven apocryphal. The wormwood-free alternative, Herbsaint, was formulated specifically to fuel New Orleans' demand for *Sazeracs*. Absinthe consumption has seen a significant revival since classic cocktail culture's rebirth in the early 2000s.[25]

Sunflower

I first tried this drink when we turned the clocks back in the fall of 2020 as a lament to the ever-decreasing hours of sunlight and chillier temperatures took hold.

The Sunflower was created by the legendary Sam Ross[26] (bartender at *Little Branch*, *Pegu Club*, *Milk & Honey*, and *Attaboy*) as a riff on the classic *Corpse Reviver No. 2* on the opposite page.

The drink showcases the woody notes of Ransom Old Tom gin, a brand that recreates the gin of the mid-to-late 1800s. In those days, gin spent a lot of time in wooden barrels traversing the Atlantic from Europe to the Americas. The woody gin and its botanicals play in unique ways with the anise-flavored rinse.

The drink may be a tad sweet for some, given the two liqueurs. You might adjust the St-Germain and Cointreau down and the gin up by ¼ oz. each.

Ingredients

¾ oz. Ransom Old Tom gin
¾ oz. Cointreau
¾ oz. St-Germain
¾ oz. lemon juice
Rinse: absinthe or Herbsaint

Directions

Prep glass with absinthe rinse. Combine all ingredients in your shaking tin. Fill with ice and shake for 15 seconds Double strain into a chilled coupe. Garnish with an expressed lemon twist.

French 75

According to cocktail historian David Wondrich, the *French 75* is the only American classic cocktail born during Prohibition.[27] That provenance, however, is a bit cloudy. In the mid-1800s, Charles Dickens wrote about enjoying a gin and Champagne cocktail that sounds suspiciously similar to what we now know as the *French 75*.

There were a few earlier drinks that carried the name of the 75-millimeter World War I field artillery gun, but the recipe took its now-classic form in *Here's How*, by Judge Jr. in 1927.[28] This recipe gained wide recognition when it was published in *The Savoy Cocktail Book* in 1930.[29] Some later cocktail books use Cognac instead of gin, as found in *The Fine Art of Mixing Drinks* (1948) by David A. Embury. Both gin and Cognac make for great versions - try them both!

Ingredients

2 oz. London dry gin or Cognac
½ oz. simple syrup
½ oz. lemon juice
4 oz. Champagne, or other sparkling wine, chilled, to top

Directions

Add gin/Cognac, syrup, and lemon juice to a shaker, add ice, and shake until chilled. Pour into a chilled coupe, Champagne flute or highball glass. Top with sparkling wine and stir gently. Garnish with a lemon twist, expressed over the top of the cocktail and dropped in.

American 46

I made this drink on November 7th, 2020 when it became clear that Joe Biden had the electoral votes to become the 46th President of the United States. My homemade peach Cognac serves as a reflection of my native state's contribution to this outcome.

1 oz. peach-infused Cognac
½ oz. lemon juice
½ oz. simple syrup
Champagne or sparkling wine to top
Garnish: lemon twist

Add all ingredients except Champagne to shaker with ice and shake. Strain into glass. Top with Champagne, stir gently. Express twist and garnish.

Cranberry 75

What else would I make on Thanksgiving? This was an ideal pre-dinner aperitivo for our quarantine Thanksgiving feast for four. Who wouldn't enjoy a *French 75* built with cranberry syrup? Follow the berry syrup recipe on page 70, and simmer until cranberries break open.

1 oz. London dry gin
½ oz. lemon juice
½ oz. cranberry syrup
2 oz. Champagne

Add all but Champagne to shaker. Shake well, then strain into Champagne flute or coupe. Top with Champagne and stir gently. Float a lemon twist and a cranberry.

Waterproof Watch

Here's a tasty combination created by Sother Teague, author of *I'm Just Here for the Drinks* and owner of *Amor y Amargo* in Brooklyn.[31] It highlights allspice liqueur and two great amari. Lacking the correct bitters, I subbed ⅛ oz. of St. Elizabeth's allspice dram.

1 ½ oz. London dry gin
¾ oz. Amaro Montenegro
¾ oz. Aperol
2 dashes Boker's or Pimento bitters
Garnish: orange twist

Directions

Combine all ingredients in a shaker. Fill tin with ice and shake for 15 seconds until well diluted. Double strain into a chilled coupe and garnish.

High Five

This drink is a riff on the *Hemingway Daiquiri* (page 39), replacing white Cuban rum with a crisp London dry gin.[30]

1½ oz. London dry gin
½ oz. Aperol
1 oz. grapefruit juice
½ oz. lime juice
½ oz. simple syrup
Garnish: grapefruit twist

Directions

Combine all ingredients in shaker. Fill tin with ice and shake for 15 seconds until well diluted. Double strain into a chilled coupe glass. Garnish.

Elder Fashioned

2 oz. Plymouth gin
¾ oz. St-Germain
2 dashes bitters (see note)
Garnish: grapefruit twist expressed

Directions

Combine all ingredients in your mixing glass. Fill glass with ice and stir for 30 seconds or until well diluted. Double strain into a chilled old-fashioned glass over a large rock. Express grapefruit twist, rub on rim of glass, and drop in.[32]

Note: Angostura is recommended, but it's great with other bitters like Fee Brothers peach or grapefruit.

Cherry Pop

Here is a gin sour I keep in frequent rotation for my evening drink that comes from the *PDT Cocktail Book*. You must use a good quality cherry for this to work!

I've tried this with many different gins, and it plays well with your classic London dry as well as softer Plymouth. The cherry taste definitely reaches the stratosphere between the Luxardo liqueur and the muddled fruit.[33]

Ingredients

2 oz. Plymouth gin
½ oz. Luxardo maraschino liqueur
1 oz. lemon juice
½ oz. simple syrup
2 Luxardo cherries (for muddling)
Garnish: 3 Luxardo cherries on pick

Directions

Add simple syrup to your shaker. Muddle two of the cherries with the syrup, then add remainder of ingredients. Shake until chilled and double strain over fresh pebble ice. Garnish with more cherries.

Cocktails & Star Trails

It amazes me that it's possible to capture images of deep space from here on planet Earth. These photos were taken by yours truly, mostly from the light-polluted city of Atlanta using digital techniques that combine hours of images into a single picture.

Astrophotography became an obsession for me back in 2017 when I picked up a used telescope to photograph the total solar eclipse that passed through north Georgia. My photo of *Bailey's Beads* is at right, the short-lived effect of sunlight shining between lunar mountains as the eclipse enters totality. This is not a hobby for the faint of heart. It's honestly one of the hardest things I've ever tried to master, calling on skills in mechanical engineering, software expertise, and my background in photojournalism.

In late 2020, Jupiter and Saturn appeared in the evening sky only 0.1 degrees apart (pictured on opposite page), an event unseen since 1226 A.D. I live-streamed the view from my telescope to friends on Facebook as I captured what was dubbed "The Great Conjunction" and celebrated with a couple of cosmic cocktails.

The *Saturn* was created in 1967 at the height of the Cold War's space race and is a gin-based tiki drink using the Caribbean spice liqueur velvet falernum with flavors of clove, lime, ginger, and almond.

The *Jupiter* is of similar vintage and is made with parfait d'amour. Lacking that somewhat obscure spirit, I subbed creme de violette plus a touch of both dry orange curaçao and vanilla.

After many chilly nights spent outdoors, it was nice to know that a warming cocktail was waiting for me inside after a late night.

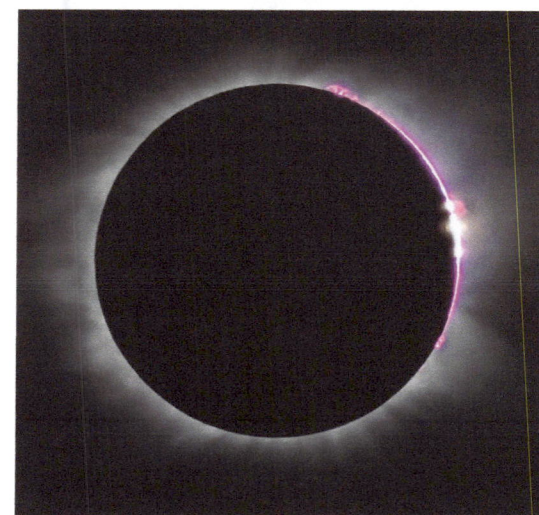

Andromeda Galaxy (top), 2017 Solar Eclipse

The Saturn

Let's be honest - this drink is all about the garnish. This flavor profile is fairly unique among tiki cocktails, as the *Saturn* features gin instead of rum. Mixed with powerful passion fruit, spicy velvet falernum, and nutty orgeat, this is a drink everyone can enjoy.

Ingredients

1½ oz. London dry gin
½ oz. passion fruit puree
½ oz. orgeat
¼ oz. John D. Taylor's velvet falernum
½ oz. orange juice
Garnish: lemon ring and cherry

Combine all ingredients in your shaking tin. Fill with ice and shake for 15 seconds. Double strain into a chilled coupe or pour over fresh pebble or crushed ice. Cut a slice of lemon and cut out inside of ring. Spear with a cocktail pick, placing a cherry in the middle. *Voila* - Saturn!

Clockwise from right: The "Great Conjunction" of Jupiter and Saturn, December 2020, the Whirlpool Galaxy, the Orion Nebula, and the total lunar eclipse of January 2019.

The Jupiter

Less well-known than the *Saturn* cocktail, the *Jupiter* is an austere but aromatic tipple. If you like an *Aviation*, you will love this drink!

Ingredients

2 oz. London dry gin
1 oz. dry white vermouth
1 tsp. dry orange curacao
1 tsp. creme de violette
2 tsp. orange juice
1 dash vanilla extract
Garnish: orange ring

Directions

Combine all ingredients in your shaking tin. Fill with ice and shake for 15 seconds. Double strain into a chilled coupe. Garnish.

The Bramble

This is a modern classic created at a bar in London's SOHO district in 1984.[34] Use caution - this goes down easy, and if you happen to be using navy-strength gin - well, you've been warned. This combination of Chambord with muddled berries, gin and lemon is among my top ten cocktails, no doubt.

Ingredients

2 oz. St. George Terroir gin
¾ oz. lemon juice
½ oz. simple syrup
¾ oz. creme de mure or Chambord
Garnish: mint, lemon, and blackberries

Directions

Add all ingredients to shaker. Add ice, shake about 15 seconds. Strain over fresh crushed ice in an old-fashioned glass. Garnish.

The easiest way to tweak the original is to swap in a different base spirit for the gin, like a dry pisco or grassy rhum agricole, or to drizzle the liqueur on top.

MIXEL MADNESS

The *Mixel* smartphone app is my bartending bible. With a catalog thousands of drinks deep, I keep track of my bottles, create custom recipes, and check other users' drink reviews. *Mixel Maximizer* calculates the most efficient additions to your stock to make the widest variety of cocktails. And I love their retro pixel-art!

Celine Fizz

The Celine Fizz is another variant from bartender Phil Ward of *Death & Company* fame, updating the classic *Ramos Gin Fizz*.[35,36] St-Germain (an elderflower liqueur) brings a lovely floral note to the velvety texture and tart-sweet effervescence of this elegant riff on a standard fizz. The original *Ramos*, notorious for taking an inordinately long time to dry shake the egg white into a foam column rising above the rim of the collins glass, is no joke. I got my upper body workout for the day when I made this one. Be sure your ingredients are as cold as possible and put the coil from your strainer in the tin when shaking. Here we use Plymouth gin, St-Germain elderflower liqueur along with the sour and sweet elements of lemon, simple syrup, and finally, that all-important egg white.

Ingredients

2 oz. Plymouth gin
½ oz. grapefruit juice
½ oz. St-Germain
¼ oz. simple syrup
¼ oz. lemon juice
1 large egg white
Dash of orange bitters
½ oz. chilled club soda
Garnish: grapefruit twist

Directions

In a cocktail shaker, combine the gin, St-Germain, fresh grapefruit juice, simple syrup, fresh lemon juice, orange bitters, shaker coil, and egg white and shake for 30-45 seconds. Add ice to the shaker and shake again for 15-20 seconds. Strain the cocktail into a chilled tall glass or flute. Place glass in freezer for ten minutes. Poke a straw down the middle of the drink and remove, then gently pour club soda down the hole. A column of foam *should* rise above the top of the glass. Pinch a grapefruit or lemon twist over the drink and rub it around the rim of the glass, drop in or discard.

Friûl Libar

The Friûl Libar's name refers to the Friluan people's political movement[37] in northeast Italy, where Amaro Nonino is produced.

Ingredients

1½ oz. Amaro Nonino Quintessentia
½ oz. Plymouth Navy Strength gin
½ oz. fresh lemon juice
¼ oz. Demerara simple syrup
2 dashes Peychaud's Bitters
Garnish: lemon twist

Directions

Combine all the ingredients in a shaker with ice. Shake until chilled. Double strain into a chilled coupe. Express twist, rub along glass rim, and notch on edge of rim.

My Tale of the Negroni

The *Negroni* was one of those drinks I wasn't sure I'd ever enjoy. Amy and I celebrated our 10th anniversary some years back with a trip to Italy. On a day trip through Chianti, our guide stopped off at a walk-up bar in a tiny village and ordered for us.

I was served what they said was a Negroni, but I couldn't stomach it. So bitter! Fast-forward a few years, and now I think they tried to serve this American a room-temperature Campari neat. Not great. The real *Negroni* is fantastic. Simultaneously bitter, sweet, and savory, this cocktail develops over time with distinct grapefruit flavors shining through, at least to my palate.

The *Negroni* was created around 1920 when Count Camillo Negroni ordered an *Americano* (sweet vermouth, Campari, and club soda) with gin swapped in for the standard soda. Orange replaced the lemon garnish, and before long, everyone was coming into the bar for a "*Negroni*."[38] Like some other classics, this is a canvas for experimentation. Using a 1:1:1 ratio of base spirit, bitter and sweet, these recipes are close cousins but very different in character.

Salute!

Unusual Negroni

Ingredients

1¼ oz. London dry gin
1 oz. Lillet Blanc
1 oz. Aperol
Garnish: grapefruit wedge

Directions

Combine all ingredients in chilled mixing glass. Fill with ice and stir 30 seconds or until well diluted and outside of glass is frosty. Strain over a large rock of ice in an old-fashioned glass and garnish.[39]

Classic Negroni

The original formula.

Ingredients

1 oz. London dry gin
1 oz. Carpano Antica sweet red vermouth
1 oz. Campari
Garnish: orange half-wheel

Directions

Combine all ingredients in chilled mixing glass. Fill with ice and stir 30 seconds or until well diluted and outside of glass is frosty. Strain over a large rock of ice in an old-fashioned glass and garnish.

Bermuda Hundred

This one is described as the love child of a *Negroni* and a *Mai Tai*.[41]

Ingredients

1½ oz. London dry gin
1½ oz. pineapple juice
¾ oz. Campari
½ oz. lime juice
½ oz. orgeat
Garnish: 1-3 cherries

Directions

Combine all ingredients in shaker, fill with ice and shake for 15 seconds. You'll want to shake extra hard to get that pineapple juice to froth nicely. Strain over a big rock in an old-fashioned glass.

Negronino

This is my favorite *Negroni* variant, featuring my favorite amaro, Nonino Quintessentia, a grappa-based liqueur with hints of caramel, vanilla, and orange.[40]

Ingredients

1 oz. London dry gin
1 oz. Carpano Antica sweet red vermouth
¾ oz. Amaro Nonino Quintessentia
2 tsp. Campari
1 tsp. simple syrup
Garnish: grapefruit wedge

Directions

Combine all ingredients in chilled mixing glass. Fill with ice and stir until well diluted and outside of glass is frosty. Strain over a large rock of ice in an old-fashioned glass and garnish.

Chapter Three:
Ho ho ho and a bottle of…

Rum is *complicated*. A sociopolitical by-product of European colonization and sugar production in the New World, it is inextricably tied to the slave trade and plantation culture across the globe. Rum production was a vital component of the so-called Triangle Trade of the Atlantic Ocean from the 16th through 19th centuries. Europe sent luxuries such as rum to Africa and exchanged these materials for humans sold into slavery. Slaves were in turn taken to the Americas, where they were paid for in rum, sugar, molasses, and other raw materials. Ultimately, rum and other products of the New World were shipped back to Europe, completing the triangle of massive human suffering. As noted in *Meehan's Bartenders Manual*,[42] the stain of slavery will never come out of the legacy of rum. Unfortunately, low wages and poor conditions for workers still persist in some corners of the world but are becoming less and less common, with producers being held accountable.

In Martin & Rebecca Cate's seminal volume on all things tiki - *Smuggler's Cove* - rum styles are broken down into no less than *twenty* categories. But fear not - most of the drinks in this volume can be made with no more than two or three types. If you enjoy this category as much as I do, *Smuggler's Cove* suggests eight core categories for your home bar.[43]

The most widely used raw material in rum production is molasses. However, in Brazil and the French Caribbean territories, rum is most often made using sugar cane juice, producing the more vegetal *rhum agricole* from Martinique (yes, with an 'h') and *cachaça* in Brazil.

It only gets more complicated from there with rums broken down by type of distillation (pot vs. column still), by age (unaged, lightly, aged, and long-aged), blended rums, and black rums. Color is a confusing aspect of rum, as coloring (often caramel) is added to both young and older rums for a consistent look. In contrast, some white rums are charcoal-filtered to remove color while retaining the taste and character of aged rum.

In addition to these styles, some countries developed other unique approaches - like Jamaican planters who used long fermentations driving aggressive flavors (see the *Honeymusk* cocktail, page 46).

Cuban rum was long a product of not the island nation but rather New England, as Cuba exported its molasses on northbound ships where the end product was distilled in the northeastern United States. By the 19th century, the Spanish saw the revenue potential for Cuban-distilled rum. They adopted local distillation using the column still, a modern approach not widely used elsewhere at that time.

In the end, rum is a spirit with a great deal of variety, with nuance defined by terroir, not unlike a fine wine. In fact, some rums from former French colonies carry an appellation *d'origine contrôlée* (AOC, "Controlled Designation of Origin,") just like Champagne or Cognac.

The Daiquiri

The daiquiri is a very refined drink and a true test of a barkeep's skill in balance, technique, and dilution. This recipe is from the late Sasha Petraske of NYC bar *Milk & Honey*. He doesn't tell us to use ¾ ounce of simple syrup - instead, he gives a range dependent on how acidic your limes taste. His book, *Regarding Cocktails*, was published posthumously by his wife, and from what I've heard, truly captures the kind, gentle, and the exacting person he was in life.[44]

2 oz. light rum
7/8 - 1 oz. fresh lime juice, to taste
¾ oz. simple syrup
Garnish: lime twist

Combine rum, juice, and simple syrup in your shaker. Add a 2-inch cube of ice and shake vigorously until the drink is sufficiently chilled and diluted. Strain into a chilled coupe. Express twist over drink, rub along rim, and garnish.

YOUR MINT HABIT

I can never keep enough fresh mint around to satisfy my cocktail experiments. I've tried growing it from seed, and while people say it grows like a weed once planted, I've been mostly unsuccessful. The best source I've found is the local farmer's market.

The Aku Aku - a daiquiri variant, page 38

Building on the Daiquiri Template

For my Savannah friends, I'll admit the word "daiquiri" evokes visions of River Street's *Wet Willies* and their dozens of whirling slushie machines. Little did I know that, in reality, this is a classic and balanced cocktail built upon a long and complex set of traditions.

And oh, the variety this cocktail offers us! Thousands of potential variations are made possible by modifying the type of rum, acid, and sweetener and the ratio between each ingredient.

The *Aku Aku* is an excellent example of an updated daiquiri. It uses a one-two combo of pineapple and peach to make a refreshing cocktail perfect for summer.

Aku Aku

Ingredients

1½ oz. Plantation 3-Stars white rum
½ oz. peach liqueur
½ oz. peach syrup (see page 70)
1 oz. lime juice
8 leaves mint
5 chunks (1-inch) fresh pineapple
or ¾ oz. pineapple juice
Garnish: mint leaf and peach slice

Directions

Muddle pineapple in drink mixer tin. Add remaining ingredients and ice, and shake vigorously for 15 seconds. Double strain into a chilled coupe. Garnish with peach slice and float a large mint leaf on the surface of the drink.[45]

38

Stiggins No. 2 Daiquiri

This drink features Plantation Spirits Stiggins Fancy Pineapple rum - a flavorful rum blend infused with ripe pineapple that tastes nothing like those mass-produced and artificially flavored versions on the bottom shelf of your local liquor store. It's also fantastic as the base for a rum old-fashioned, but is equally marvelous in this daiquiri.[47]

2 oz. Plantation Spirits pineapple rum
¼ oz. yellow Chartreuse
¾ oz. lime juice
2 dashes Angostura bitters

Combine ingredients in tin, add ice and shake for 15 seconds. Double strain into a chilled coupe. Garnish with a lime twist or wedge.

Hemingway Daiquiri

Also known as the "*Papa Doble*," the mythology suggests that Ernest Hemingway asked for this specification at Havana's *El Floridita* bar. He was said to have consumed sixteen of these at one sitting.[48] The man was a monster! Your palate may prefer to add a touch of rich (2:1) simple syrup for balance.

3 oz. Havana Club white rum
1 bar spoon Luxardo Maraschino liqueur
½ oz. lime juice
1 oz. grapefruit juice
Optional: ½ oz. rich simple syrup
Garnish: lime wheel, cherries

Combine all ingredients in shaker, fill with ice and shake for 15 seconds. Double strain into chilled coupe and garnish with a few Luxardo cherries and lime.

French Daiquiri

This is a riff on the *French Martini* using Chambord berry liqueur alongside the unaged funk of Jamaican overproof rum and grassy notes from French-style rhum agricole.[46] It's a flavor bomb.

¾ oz. Clement Blue rhum agricole
½ oz. J. Wray & Nephew over proof rum
½ oz. Chambord liqueur
1½ oz. pineapple juice
½ oz. lime juice
2 dashes orange bitters
Garnish: lime wedge

Shake all ingredients with ice and double strain into a chilled coupe. Garnish.

Lauwiliwilinukunuku'oi'oi

Don't try to pronounce this one. This is the Hawaiian name for the longnose butterflyfish and holds the record for the longest name of any native species on the islands.[50] You can also substitute two ounces of gin for rum for to create another great drink, the *Humuhumunukunukuapua'a*!

1 oz. Plantation 3 Stars white rum
1 oz. Rhum J.M. VO rhum agricole
¾ oz. lemon juice
¾ oz. unsweetened pineapple juice
½ oz. orgeat
2 dashes Peychaud's Bitters
Garnish: cherries

Add all ingredients to shaker with 8 oz. crushed ice. Shake briefly and open pour into a double rocks glass. Garnish with cherries.

Lost Lake

Oh, boy is this a fine drink, a variation on another Campari tiki drink and the namesake beverage of the *Lost Lake* tiki bar in Chicago. I used two types of passion fruit: Chinola, a passion fruit liqueur I highly recommend, and the pulp from half of a fresh passion fruit found at my local farmers market.

2 oz. Smith & Cross Navy Strength rum
¼ oz. Campari
¼ oz. maraschino liqueur
¾ oz. lime juice
¾ oz. Chinola passion fruit liqueur
½ fresh passion fruit pulp
½ oz. pineapple juice
Garnish: pineapple wedge & leaf

Add all ingredients to shaker with 1 oz. crushed ice. Whip shake briefly and double-strain into a footed pilsner glass over fresh crushed or pebble ice. Garnish with pineapple wedge and leaf.

Jamaican Milk Punch

This version of the drink comes from San Francisco's *Smuggler's Cove* menu, updating a traditional recipe with bourbon that the 1873 *Brooklyn Daily Eagle* called "the surest thing in the world to get drunk on."[49] They weren't wrong.

1 oz. Smith & Cross overproof rum
1 oz. whole milk
1 oz. heavy cream
½ oz. 2:1 Demerara syrup
6 drops vanilla extract
1 dash Angostura bitters
Garnish: grated nutmeg

Combine all ingredients and shake for 30 seconds. Strain into a double old-fashioned glass over fresh cracked ice. Grate a touch of fresh nutmeg over the top.

Authentically Inauthentic:
The Rise, Fall and Rebirth of Tiki

Tiki is problematic. Born in the 1930s, the tiki movement contributed incredible creations to the craft of the cocktail. A mash-up of iconography from the Pacific Islands, rum from the Caribbean, and food from Asia, tiki was an American-made escape from the hardships of the Great Depression to an imaginary tropical paradise.

The movement was a worldwide phenomenon for decades, but by the 1970s had begun to fade away in the face of mass-produced ingredients and the disco scene. But all things old are new again, and the cocktail renaissance of the early 2000s saw a return to the craftsmanship and complexity underlying the best of tiki cocktails.

The challenge we face today is recognizing that tiki should be viewed in the context of the movement's ignorance of indigenous culture, misuse of religious symbolism, and a generally colonialist view of the entire Pacific Rim. Recent movements like "Doom Tiki" replace exploitative imagery with death-metal, rockabilly, or even sci-fi themes and are early steps toward fixing what's broken. Enjoy the drinks, but know your history.

Fogg Cutter

Indeed not the simplest tiki classic; this is one of a handful of tiki classics with its own namesake glassware (pictured below). I haven't picked up any Fogg Cutter mugs yet (we don't have room for much more glassware!), but it sure is lovely.

1 oz. London dry gin
1 oz. aged rum
1 oz. Cognac
2 oz. lime juice
1 oz. orgeat
½ oz. Amontillado sherry
½ oz. orange curaçao
½ oz. simple syrup
1 dash Angostura
Garnish: tropical assortment (edible flowers, fruit, umbrellas, etc.)

Combine all ingredients in shaker. Add an ounce of crushed ice, whip shake, and then strain into a tiki mug over fresh crushed ice. Fill with more crushed ice, garnish and enjoy!

Captain's Grog

To make a Captain's Grog, combine all ingredients with an ounce of crushed ice into a mixing tin. Whip shake briefly and pour into a chilled tiki mug or double old-fashioned glass. Top with more crushed ice. Garnish with mint, umbrella, and reusable straw.

¾ oz. Gosling Black rum
¾ oz. Plantation 3-Stars rum
¾ oz. Chairman's Reserve Forgotten Cask
½ oz. orange curaçao
½ oz. velvet falernum
½ oz. lime juice
½ oz. grapefruit juice
½ oz. maple syrup (or honey syrup)
3 drops vanilla extract
3 drops almond extract
1 oz. club soda
Garnish: mint

Fogg Cutter

41

Ferrel's Hurricane

I've always been a weather geek, so it was only natural that I joined The Weather Company a few years ago to direct its advertising technology practice. Every time a land-falling hurricane threatens, it's all hands on deck to fulfill our mission of keeping people out of harm's way. After some of these storms, I would turn to this New Orleans classic. Here's the best variant I've found to date, created by Ferrel Dugas, (former) Bar Chef at *Commander's Palace* in New Orleans.[51]

The drink's secret ingredient is fassionola syrup, a key to tiki classics like the *Hurricane* and the *Cobra's Fang*. I'm aware of only one commercial source, and it's only made in a limited run once a year when the required local produce is in season. It includes strawberries from Ponchatoula, Louisiana, fresh pineapple, mango, passionfruit, lime peels, and hibiscus flower.

¾ oz. Plantation Fiji Estate rum
¾ oz. Havana Club white rum
½ oz. Galliano liqueur
1 oz. Cocktail & Sons fassionola syrup (see Resources, page 72)
¾ oz. lemon juice
¾ oz. lime juice
8 drops Angostura or Bittercube Jamaican #1
Garnish: pineapple wedge, cherries, nutmeg

Add all the ingredients to a shaker and add a half-handful of crushed ice. Whip shake until ice is dissolved and strain into a tall glass filled with fresh pebble or crushed ice. Garnish with an inside-out cocktail umbrella, a pineapple wedge, cherries, and a dusting of grated nutmeg.

KNOW YOUR INGREDIENTS: ORGEAT

Orgeat is an almond syrup. The best commercial option comes from Hand Made Foods (via Amazon), but you can also make it at home. Recipe on page 70.

Freydis

For the *Freydis*, I used a liberated bottle of 1960s-era Scandinavian aquavit from my in-law's house. It adds a decidedly sharp caraway/rye undertone to the flavor party.[52]

¾ oz. light rum
¾ oz. aquavit
½ oz. Aperol
½ oz. orgeat
¼ oz. peach liqueur or peach syrup
Garnish: mint sprig

Combine all ingredients in shaker. Add a handful of ice and shake for 15 seconds until well diluted. Strain into a hurricane glass over fresh crushed or pebble ice. Garnish.

Pina Colada

An instant vacation, updated to reduce the sweetness and bring the rum to the forefront.

1¾ oz. Plantation 3 Stars white rum
¼ oz. Lemon Hart 151 Demerara rum
1½ oz. pineapple juice
1½ oz. House Coco (4:1 Coco Lopez to unsweetened coconut milk)
1 oz. simple syrup

Combine all ingredients in shaker. Add a handful of ice and shake for 15 seconds until well diluted. Strain into a parrot mug - or whatever you have - over fresh crushed or pebble ice. Garnish.

Artichoke Hold

This is a bitter take on the *Mai Tai* (page 45). The drink combines three key ingredients for balance: Cynar, an artichoke-based Italian amaro, funky overproof Jamaican rum, and bartender's ketchup (aka St-Germain) to make a very balanced bittersweet version of the classic.[53]

¾ oz. Smith & Cross overproof rum
¾ oz. Cynar, plus ¼ oz. for garnish
½ oz. St-Germain
¾ oz. lime juice
½ oz. orgeat
Mint sprigs as garnish

Add all ingredients to a shaker with a small amount of ice. Whip shake until chilled. Strain over fresh crushed ice in an old-fashioned glass. Top with more ice to form a cone and garnish with a mint sprig. Drizzle ¼ oz. Cynar over the top of the cone. Garnish with a forest of mint.

The Mighty Mai Tai

During the lockdown, some of our earliest adventures out of the house were a few socially distanced camping excursions with trusted friends. On one trip, I decided to create *Mai Tais* for a crowd from a great recipe I found on the *Lost Tiki Lounge*[54] website.

The tricky issue here is that proportions don't scale linearly, as some ingredients (e.g., bitters or strong syrups like orgeat & ginger) are amplified as they increase in quantity. I suggest using ½ the amount of these types of components, testing and tasting as you go.

First, I assemble the spirits I can mix well in advance. Next up are the "small but potent" elements like syrup and aromatics, which I bottle separately. Finally, there's the citrus. Ideally, you would squeeze to order but can get away with extracting the juice a few hours ahead of time and storing it on ice until ready to serve.

You can use a combination of different rums here. Still, the best approximation of the original *Trader Vic's Mai Tai* is Denizen Merchant Reserve, a custom blend of Jamaican rum and Rhum Grande Arôme de Martinique.

Any time in the week leading up to your event, mix "base" ingredients in a large container, decant into bottles, and store them in the fridge. Pour "small but potent" ingredients into a small jug, cover, and place in refrigerator.

On the day of your event, squeeze limes as close to party time possible, bottling juice and storing it in the fridge. Make sure you keep all your squeezed lime halves chilled for garnish.

Ten minutes before guests arrive, take out lime halves, lime juice, and pre-mixes, giving the bottles a good shake in the process. To make each serving, add 2½ ounces of your "base" pre-mix, ¾ ounces of the "small but potent" mix, and one ounce of fresh lime juice.

Add ice and shake vigorously for 15-20 seconds. Strain into a double old-fashioned glass over crushed ice. Garnish with a sprig of (freshly slapped) mint and drop in one of the lime halves. Add an umbrella and serve!

Mai Tais for a Crowd

1.5 servings for 8 guests = 12
Total volume = 51 oz/1.5 Litre
Base volume = 30 oz/887 ml
Small but potent = 9 oz/266 ml

Base Ingredients
24 oz. Denizen Merchant Reserve Blended rum
6 oz. Pierre Ferrand dry orange curaçao

Perishable Ingredients
12 oz. Fresh lime juice

Small but Potent
6 oz. Orgeat syrup
3 oz. Simple syrup

Mai Tai

The single-serving recipe for Trader Vic's classic of the tiki movement.

2 oz. Denizen Merchant Reserve rum
½ oz. orange curaçao
1 oz. fresh lime juice
½ oz. orgeat
¼ oz. simple syrup
Garnish: Mint sprig and spent half lime

Combine all ingredients in tin, then whip-shake with a half-handful of crushed ice. Strain into a double old-fashioned glass or tiki mug over fresh crushed ice. Garnish with a sprig of (bruised) mint and drop in one of the lime halves.

Bikini Atoll

Here's an herbal Mai Tai on steroids. This tiki drink has so many things that add up to much more than the sum of its parts.[55]

1 oz. Smith & Cross Jamaican rum
½ oz. green Chartreuse
½ oz. John D. Taylor velvet falernum
½ oz. Pierre Ferrand Dry orange curaçao
½ oz. orgeat
1 oz. fresh lime juice
Garnish: mint sprig

Add all ingredients to shaker. Add ice, shake about 15 seconds. Double strain over fresh ice in a double old-fashioned glass. Garnish with slapped mint sprig.

45

El Presidente

I enjoyed this classic Cuban cocktail during one of the presidential debates in early Fall 2020. First published in 1915, the drink uses blanc vermouth, a decidedly non-Cuban spirit that brings a light sweetness along with vanilla.[57]

1½ oz. Bacardi 8 gold rum
½ oz. Dolin vermouth blanc
½ oz. Pierre Ferrand dry orange curaçao
½ oz. lime juice
1 bar spoon grenadine
Garnish: orange twist and/or cherry

Combine all ingredients in shaker. Add ice and shake for 15 seconds until well diluted. Strain into a chilled coupe glass. Express twist and garnish with orange and/or cherry.

Between the Sheets

For this drink from *Death & Company*,[56] I used one of my absolute favorite rums, St. Lucia's Chairman's Reserve Forgotten Casks aged rum. It's a great sipper and mixer.

1 oz. Chairman's Reserve Forgotten Casks
1 oz. Pierre Ferrand 1840 Cognac
¾ oz. Pierre Ferrand Dry orange curaçao
¾ oz. lemon juice
1 tsp. Demerara gomme syrup (see pg 70)
Garnish: flamed orange peel

Combine all ingredients in shaker. Add ice to tin and shake for 15 seconds until well diluted. Double strain into a chilled coupe glass. Carefully hold peel over drink, ignite lighter and express oils from orange peel through flame. Drop peel into cocktail and serve.

Honeymusk

My first take on this drink I found at *KindredCocktails.com*,[58] which split the base between a blended white rum and an overproof Jamaican white. I eventually settled on a version using Smith & Cross Navy Strength rum, so-called because its alcohol content is so high, gunpowder could still ignite if a barrel of rum happened to spill in the hold. This rum is full of funk or "hogo," a term that stems from the French "*haut gout*," which refers to slightly tainted meat or other strong yet desirable flavors.[59] Trust me.

1½ oz. Smith & Cross Jamaican rum
1 oz. lemon juice
1 oz. pineapple syrup
¾ oz. Cynar

Combine all in shaker. Add ice and shake for 15 seconds until well diluted. Double strain into a chilled coupe glass. Garnish with lemon wheel.

Morgenthaler's Eggnog

There are many competing theories on creating the best eggnog. If you have the patience, Alton Brown's 3-week recipe[60] from his website is an excellent example of an aged approach (although some suggest aging for a year!). Jeffrey Morgenthaler, author of *The Bar Book: Elements of Cocktail Technique,* serves an añejo tequila version at his bar *Clyde Common* in Portland, Oregon. The version below is more traditional and also comes from Morgenthaler.[61] You may find the recipe a little on the sweet side, so try starting with 1½ or 1 ounce of his recommended sugar and increase if desired. And to try his alternate version, replace the Cognac and rums with 2 ounces añejo tequila and 2½ ounces Amontillado sherry.

Ingredients - Serves Two

2 eggs, whole
3 oz. powdered sugar
2 oz. Pierre Ferrand 1840 Cognac
1 oz. Smith & Cross Navy Strength Jamaican rum
1 oz. spiced rum (Sailor Jerry or Kraken are quality brands)
6 oz. whole milk
4 oz. heavy cream
Garnish: grated fresh nutmeg, cinnamon stick

Directions

Beat eggs in blender for 1 minute at medium speed. Slowly add sugar and blend for an additional minute. With blender still running, add Cognac, rum, milk, and cream until combined. Chill thoroughly to allow flavors to meld. You can decide to let this age for a day, a week, a few months, or, well - you get the picture. Serve up in chilled glasses with fresh nutmeg on top and a cinnamon stick.

Top-Notch Volcano

Oh, this brings me back to my college days in metro Boston. The *Top-Notch Volcano* is a single-serving version of the (in)famous *Scorpion Bowl*.[62] I enjoyed more than a few of these at the tongue-in-cheek named *Peking Tom's* bar near Boston's Prudential Tower, as well as the *Hong Kong Restaurant* in Harvard Square. There's nary a drink less suited for quarantine than a bowl of hooch, but this is fine for consumption at home during quarantine!

Ingredients

1 oz. dark rum
1 oz. light rum
¼ oz. Luxardo maraschino liqueur
1 oz. lime juice
1 oz. pineapple juice
¼ oz. passion fruit juice
¾ oz. Demerara or pineapple syrup 2:1
Garnish: pineapple wedge or passion fruit half

Directions

Add all ingredients to shaker. Add ice, then shake for about 15 seconds. Strain over fresh crushed ice in a tiki mug or collins glass. Garnish.

OLD GROGRAM

The term "Grog" comes from the nickname "Old Grog," given to 18th century British Admiral Vernon. He was known to wear a cloak made of grogram, a coarse fabric of silk and wool stiffened with gum. In 1740, he ordered sailors' daily rum ration be diluted from 116-proof with lime juice and sugar. And so Grog was born.[63]

3 Dots and A Dash

Crafted during World War II, this patriotic tiki drink refers to Morse Code for the letter V, as in "V for Victory!"[64]

Ingredients

2 oz. Denizen Merchant's Reserve rum
¼ oz. John D. Taylor's velvet falernum
¼ oz. St. Elizabeth allspice dram
½ oz. honey syrup (1:1 honey to water)
½ oz. lime juice
½ oz. orange juice
1 dash Angostura bitters
Garnish: 3 maraschino cherries above one pineapple chunk on a cocktail pick

Directions

Combine all ingredients in a shaker with ice. Shake until chilled. Strain over fresh ice in a tiki mug or tall glass. Garnish.

Beachbum's Own

This tasty tiki drink comes from *Latitude 29*, a popular tiki joint in New Orleans. It starts with a mix of rums, adds spice and vanilla from Spanish Licor 43, rounded out with three different juices.

Ingredients

1½ oz. Plantation 3-Stars white rum
1¼ oz. Lemon Hart 151 overproof dark rum
¾ oz. Licor 43
¾ oz. passion fruit juice
¾ oz. pineapple juice
¾ oz. lemon juice

Directions

Combine all the ingredients in a shaker with ice. Shake until chilled. Strain over fresh ice in a tiki mug or tall glass.

Golden Gun

This is another great drink from *Smuggler's Cove* in San Francisco. I amped this up with my homemade pineapple syrup. It's also a great excuse to buy a good apricot liqueur like this one from Rothman & Winter.

Ingredients

2 oz. Denizen Merchant's Reserve rum
    or 1 oz. dark rum and 1 oz. light rum
½ oz. Rothman and Winter Apricot liqueur
½ oz. pineapple syrup
½ oz. grapefruit juice
¾ oz. lime juice
2 dashes Angostura bitters

Directions

Combine all the ingredients in a shaker with ice. Shake until chilled. Strain over fresh ice in a tiki mug or tall glass.

Rita's 'rita

I created my take on the classic margarita blend of sour, sweet and savory, and named it for my mom, Rita. Here I'm splitting the sour base using lime, orange, and lemon juices. Using mixology mad-scientist Dave Arnold's tip from his book, *Liquid Intelligence*, I add a touch of saline solution.[66] Salt is a flavor enhancer - try it in pretty much any cocktail!

Ingredients

2 oz. tequila blanco (Casamigos or Fortaleza)
1 oz. Cointreau
¼ oz. blue agave syrup
¾ oz. lime juice
¼ oz. orange juice
¼ oz. lemon juice
4 drops 20% saline (20g salt, 80g water)
Garnish: lime wedge

Directions

Combine all ingredients in your shaker. Add ice and shake 10-15 seconds. Double strain into a double Old-fashioned glass over a big rock. Garnish with a lime wedge.

Rita's 'rita

Chapter Four:
One tequila, two tequila, three tequila...

Agave comes from the Greek word for royalty, *agavacea*, which in turn refers to a family of succulent plants. Both mezcal and tequila are made from agave, so what's the difference?

While mezcal can be produced from up to fifty different species of the agave plant, tequila can be made from just one, *agave tequilana weber*, or weber blue agave. Most mezcals are roasted in underground pits, providing their distinctive smoky note. In the Mexican town of Tequila, a unique style of mezcal developed in which agave was steamed in ovens to create a clean, vegetal flavor. Early in the 20th century, people recognized that the mezcal style from this region was quite different, with more complexity and smoothness. Now, we know that form of mezcal simply as "tequila."[65]

The smokiness of some mezcal is still a taste I'm trying to love, but I'm devoted to the subtle grassy notes that a good tequila brings on its own or mixed into a cocktail. A word to the wise - buy a good quality tequila. Avoid your "mixto" tequilas - those are not 100% agave and can, by U.S. law, contain up to 49% other sources of sugar for fermentation. You can thank those college headaches on poor-quality mixtos!

PARTY TIP

Necessity is the mother of invention. For Noah's socially distanced backyard Bar mitzvah party in November 2020, I prebatched individual servings of *Dos Besitos* in Mason jars that each guest could shake themselves. Recipe, page 55.

Dos Besitos

Ty Cobbler

Here's a sophisticated take on a tequila drink with a pleasant dryness balanced by the dark sweetness of cherries.[67] I've enjoyed the *Ty Cobbler* with a blanco tequila, but an aged reposado works as well.

2 oz. blanco or reposado tequila
½ oz. Cynar
¼ oz. simple syrup
3 Amarena cherries
2 dashes Fee Brothers Aztec chocolate bitters
Garnish: orange wheel

Add all to shaker. Add ice, shake about 15 seconds. Double strain over fresh crushed ice in a double old-fashioned glass. Garnish.

Santa Rosa

This drink comes from *Kirkland Tap* in Sommerville, Massachusetts.[69] Carpano Antica or Lillet Blanc are both great alternatives to the Cocchi Rosa of the original formula.

1½ oz. tequila blanco
¼ oz. Carpano Antica sweet vermouth
        or Lillet Blanc or Coccchi Rosa
½ oz. peach liqueur
½ oz. lemon juice
¼ oz. agave syrup
Garnish: lemon twist

Combine all the ingredients in a shaker with ice. Shake until chilled. Double strain into a chilled coupe. Express oils from twist, rub along glass rim and garnish.

Malibu

This is a delicious tequila, lime and grapefruit drink softened by fortified floral wine, Lillet Blanc.[68]

2 oz. tequila blanco
1 oz. pisco (or rhum agricole blanc)
½ oz. Lillet Blanc
1 tsp. Campari
1 oz. Pamplemousse liqueur
1 oz. grapefruit syrup (recipe, pg. 70)
1½ oz. lime juice
2 drops 20% saline (20g salt, 80g water)
Garnish: grapefruit wedge or candied peel

Combine all the ingredients in a shaker with ice. Shake until chilled. Double strain into a chilled coupe. Garnish.

Oaxacan Old-Fashioned

Named for the Mexican state from which many of the smokiest of mezcals hail, this drink mixes reposado tequila, which is lightly aged in oak, with the super-smoky flavors of mezcal.[70] For a smoke-phobic drinker like myself, I've reduced the mezcal to a 3:1 ratio with the tequila base, creating a fine gateway into the world of smoky agave spirits.

Ingredients

1½ oz. reposado tequila
½ oz. mezcal
1 teaspoon agave nectar
2 dashes Angostura bitters
Garnish: flamed orange peel

Directions

Add the tequila, mezcal, agave nectar, and Angostura bitters in an old-fashioned glass with one large ice cube, and stir until well-chilled. Flame an orange peel over the top of the drink to express oils, then garnish with the peel.

MEZCAL MADNESS

Most quality mezcals on the market tend to be costly. One introduction to the smoky category of agave spirits is Del Maguey VIDA. It's still handcrafted from a single village but is half the price of the rest of the Del Maguey line. It's ideal for mixing or sipping neat.

Cantarito

Drinking a cocktail out of a clay planter? Well, yes, I'd love to! I first enjoyed a *Cantarito* at the now-defunct *El Mexicano*, an authentic Mexican joint in our neighborhood. And yes, it was served in a shallow clay pot with multiple straws. Basically, it's a Mexican-inspired *Scorpion Bowl* (see page 48). In the end, the *Cantarito* is a dressed-up margarita, using various fruit juices and sweetened by soda. You can use the less-sugary Squirt or even Topo Chico grapefruit flavor, although you might need to add a ¼ ounce of simple syrup for balance.[71]

Ingredients

2 oz. blanco tequila
1¼ oz. orange juice
¾ oz. grapefruit juice
¾ oz. lime juice
4 oz. grapefruit soda (Jaritos or others, see above)
4 drops 20% saline (20g salt, 80g water)
Garnish: Tajin spice blend, plus wedges of grapefruit, orange, and lime

Directions

Add all ingredients but soda and garnish to shaker. Add ice and shake for about 15 seconds. Strain over fresh ice in a collins glass. Add soda, stir gently. Garnish with a sprinkle of Tajin spice blend and citrus wedges.

LEMON FRESH

I go through a bag of a dozen each of lemons and limes every two weeks. To keep them fresh, I refrigerate them in airtight zip-top bags. A paper towel in the bag will help absorb excess moisture and keep them fresh longer. Bonus: cocktail wonks say refrigerated citrus produce the most juice when squeezed.

Dos Besitos

For the small and socially distanced party we held in honor of our son Noah the night he became a Bar mitzvah, I knew I needed to come up with a tasty cocktail for the couple of families who joined us in our backyard celebration. *Dos Besitos* (literally "two kisses") fit the bill.[72]

Single Serving

1 oz. aged tequila
1 oz. blanco tequila
¾ oz. pineapple juice
½ oz. lime juice
¼ oz. agave nectar
1 tsp. grenadine

For Party of 8

8 Guests at 1.5 Servings each = 12 Total Servings
Total volume = 42 oz.

Small but Potent: 3 oz.

2 oz. agave nectar
1 oz. grenadine

Base Pre-Mix: 24 oz.

12 oz. Casamigos Anejo tequila
12 oz. Casamigos Blanco tequila

Perishable Ingredients: 15 oz.

6 oz. lime juice
9 oz. pineapple juice

The week before your event, mix "base" ingredients in a large container, then decant them into bottles. Pour "small but potent" ingredients into a small container. Store containers in the fridge.

On the day of the party, squeeze fruit as close to party time as possible, bottling the juice and storing it in the fridge. I recommend bottled cold-press pineapple juice if you can't extract your own. Ten minutes before guests arrive, take out juices and pre-mixes, and give the bottles a good shake.

For our event, I split the drinks into individual small Mason jars (pictured at right). Simply combine all elements and divide among the jars. Then let guests add ice and shake when ready to drink.

The Paloma

Grapefruit and tequila go together like peanut butter and jelly, and the *Paloma* is a cocktail that lets this pairing shine. I discovered the vodka-based version of this (the *Greyhound*) at a neighborhood joint, *Ziba's*. I started making this tequila-based version (because vodka is boring) at home during the pandemic before restaurants began reopening.

Fresh

Tart

Ingredients

2 oz. Casamigos blanco tequila
4 oz. grapefruit juice
¼ oz. lime juice
Top with soda (see note below) to taste
Garnish: lime/grapefruit wedges

Directions

Add all ingredients but soda to shaker. Add ice, shake 10-15 seconds until well chilled. Pour over fresh ice in a collins glass. Top with soda, garnish with lime and/or grapefruit wedge.

Note: For a drier cocktail, top with club soda or grapefruit Topo Chico. For a sweeter taste, use ginger ale or Jaritos grapefruit soda.

Avion de Papel

If you haven't already sampled one, I suggest you turn back to my chapter on whiskey and give my favorite drink in this book a try - the *Paper Plane* (page 17). That drink is equal parts bourbon, bittersweet Aperol, lemon juice, and Amaro Nonino Quintessentia. Here, we go with a Mexican-influenced version, subbing tequila for bourbon.[73] It has no grapefruit, but you would swear that was half the ingredients. *Avion de Papel* is super refreshing and a worthy variant of a modern classic.

Ingredients

¾ oz. Forteleza Blanco tequila
¾ oz. Aperol
¾ oz. Amaro Nonino Quintessentia
¾ oz. lemon juice
Garnish: lemon twist or slice

Directions

Add all ingredients to shaker. Add ice and shake for about 15 seconds. Double strain into a chilled coupe. Garnish with a lemon slice or twist.

SHAKE, SHAKE, SHAKE

I recommend using one large (2-inch) ice cube and a couple of "normal" refrigerator cubes for shaken cocktails. The big cube provides aeration while the smaller provides dilution.

Chapter Five: Sweet, bitter & in-between

Liqueurs and brandies are amazingly diverse spirit categories often combined to create some of the most classic cocktails.

Cognac is an elegant spirit and part of the broader category of brandy. The word brandy comes from the Dutch "*brandewijn*" or "burned wine" and refers to the process of distilling wine into brandy or *eau de vie*. Cognac, like tequila, is named for the town from which it hails. Its unique approach to brandy distillation was legendary as early as the 16th century. In 1909, Cognac received protected certification, thus solidifying it as one of the world's most sought-after spirits.[74]

In Colonial-era America, brandy was distilled by "jacking," a process where hard cider was left to freeze outdoors in winter. As the water froze, it left behind a higher-proof spirit called Applejack. In Peru, the unaged spirit we now know as pisco is also created with a unique process. Unlike brandy, pisco is unaged and never touches a wooden barrel. Sweeter European grape varietals, initially introduced to Peru by Spanish colonizers, are briefly fermented and then distilled into this earthy spirit.[75]

Liqueurs are the broadest category of spirits. European monks first created these libations for medicinal purposes based on the health benefits of local flora. Chartreuse, Bénédictine, and Campari recipes are closely guarded secrets, with some unchanged since the 1500s. While it's known that 130 ingredients are used to make Chartreuse, only two people at a time know the secret formula.

Like Atlanta's own Coca-Cola, what was once medicinal is now enjoyed for more recreational purposes. Some of these liqueurs are strikingly bitter: Suze, from France, derives its extremely dry profile from macerated gentian root, while others, like Luxardo's maraschino cherry liqueur, are often used in place of simple syrup.

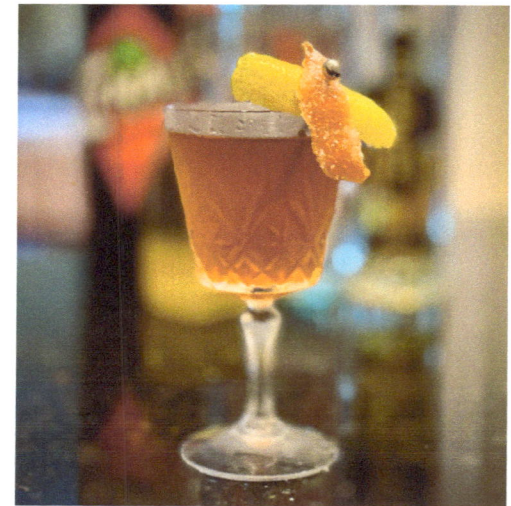

Lady Amaro

A tasty contrast of bitter Cynar and floral St-Germain defines this gin cocktail from *Bambara* in Cambridge, Massachusetts.[76]

Ingredients

1½ oz. London dry gin
½ oz. St-Germain
½ oz. Cynar
½ oz. grapefruit syrup
Garnish: candied grapefruit peel, lemon twist

Directions

Combine ingredients in shaker. Add ice, shake well for 10-15 seconds, then double strain into a chilled coupe. Garnish with candied grapefruit peel (dried after creating grapefruit oleo saccharum, page 70) as well as a fresh lemon twist.

Champs-Élysées

This classic takes the *Sidecar* and turns it on its head, replacing dry curaçao's citrus notes with the herbaceous flavor bomb of green Chartreuse. However, the drink remains balanced with the Chartreuse complementing and not competing with the other ingredients.

I first discovered this drink during a socially distanced get-together with Joel & Rachel Silverman, dear friends who helped keep our family sane (and vice versa) during the depths of the lockdown.

Joel has a comprehensive collection of cocktail books and spirits. Tasked with picking a pre-dinner cocktail, I turned to his books and found the late Sasha Petraske's book *Regarding Cocktails*.[77] The recipe for this delightful drink was perfect for an alfresco dinner on the Silverman's porch.

Ingredients

2 oz. Pierre Ferrand 1840 Cognac
½ oz. green Chartreuse
¾ oz. lemon juice
½ oz. simple syrup 2:1
1 dash Angostura bitters
Garnish: lemon twist

Directions

Shake all ingredients with ice for 10-15 seconds and double strain into a coupe. Express lemon twist and garnish.

Pears n' Apples

Brandy just feels like Fall, and the addition of some homemade pear syrup and Woodford Reserve cherry aromatic bitters come together in this original drink I created last year.

Ingredients

2 oz. Clear Creek Distillery 8-year apple brandy
1½ tsp. pear syrup (recipe, pg. 70)
1 dash Woodford Reserve cherry aromatic bitters
1 dash Angostura bitters
Garnish: pear and apple fan

Directions

Add all ingredients to mixing glass. Stir 40 seconds or until well diluted. Strain over a large rock in a chilled old-fashioned glass. Garnish.

HOMEMADE?

You can create your own liqueurs at home. Combine equal amounts of a base (brandy is typical), water, sugar, and sliced fruit (pear/peach), skin and all. Then add seasoning - a vanilla bean is excellent. Seal in a jar, store in a cool place and give a gentle shake once daily. Let age for a few days to a few weeks, tasting as you go. Strain and bottle.

Bananarac

The original *Sazerac* was made with brandy, but American rye stepped in after a late 1800s blight devastated European vineyards. This variant splits the base and adds a high-quality banana liqueur for a surprising twist.

1 oz. Pierre Ferrand 1840 Cognac
1 oz. Rittenhouse 100-proof rye
½ oz. Tempus Fugit crème de banane
¾ tsp. Demerara syrup
1 dash Peychauds or Angostura bitters
Rinse of St. George Spirits absinthe verte
Garnish: lemon twist

Prepare chilled double old-fashioned glass by rinsing with a touch of absinthe or a spray from an atomizer. Add ingredients to mixing glass, add ice and stir for 30-40 seconds. Strain into an old-fashioned glass. Serve up or over a 2-inch ice cube, express twist, and discard.

Sazerac

This recipe is a nod to the original which used Cognac alone. Over time, it shifted to rye whiskey. Here, we split the base by using both.[79]

1¼ oz. rye whiskey
1¼ oz. Cognac
Absinthe, to rinse
1 sugar cube
½ tsp. cold water
3 dashes Peychaud's bitters
2 dashes Angostura bitters
Garnish: lemon peel

Prep old-fashioned glass with absinthe, discarding excess. In mixing glass, muddle the sugar cube, water, Peychaud's, and Angostura. Add rye and Cognac, fill with ice and stir until well-chilled. Strain into the prepared glass. Twist the lemon peel over the drink's surface, then garnish with peel.

Y Control

This is a play on the classic *Brandy Daisy* cocktail, adding complexity with herbal liqueur and pineapple syrup.[78]

1½ oz. Pierre Ferrand 1840 Cognac
¾ oz. lime juice
½ oz. pineapple syrup
1 tsp. yellow Chartreuse
1 tsp. Maraschino liqueur
Garnish: lemon twist

Add all ingredients to shaker. Add ice, shake about 15 seconds. Double strain into a chilled coupe. Express twist and garnish.

Improved Japanese Cocktail

Sweet

Boozy

This is a twist on the *Japanese Cocktail*, which dates back to the mid-1860s. Cocktail historian David Wondrich, author of books *Imbibe!* and *Punch*, suggests that the name of the original stemmed from a Japanese diplomat who was a frequent visitor to a bar operated by the father of American mixology, Jerry Thomas. The original drink was immortalized in Thomas' *How to Mix Drinks or The Bon-Vivant's Companion* (1862). The key "improvement" here comes by way of adding lemon juice and Peychaud's bitters.

Ingredients

2 oz. Pierre Ferrand Ambre Cognac
1 oz. lemon juice
1 oz. orgeat
3 dashes Peychaud's bitters
Garnish: lemon and/or orange twist

Directions

Stir ingredients over ice, then pour over a large rock in a double old-fashioned glass. Express twists and garnish.

Fire in the Orchard

After a freezing evening of astronomy, I thought "Fire in the Orchard" would fit the bill. Created at *No 9. Park* in Boston[80], the fire comes from Del Maguey single-village origin mezcal, while apple brandy and pear liqueur supply the fruit. Lemon and agave syrup give balance to the mezcal's smoke.

Ingredients

1¼ oz. apple brandy
¼ oz. Del Maguey Vida mezcal
½ oz. Mathilde pear liqueur
¾ oz. Lillet Blanc
½ oz. lemon juice
¼ oz. agave syrup (1:1)

Directions

Add all ingredients to shaker, fill with ice. Shake 10-15 seconds, then double strain into a chilled coupe glass.

Fresh

Smoky

DOUBLE STRAINING

We don't strain just to hold back pulp and seeds but to give a shaken cocktail the smoothest texture possible. By using both a hawthorne and a small extra fine-mesh strainer, we keep ice shards out of the drink and avoid ruining the smooth texture we created during shaking. See *Resources*, page 72.

Velvet Club

Here's a modern update to the *Velvet Glove*, a classic cocktail dating back to 1937. Found in *The PDT Cocktail Book*,[81] this version features more balanced proportions. It uses white crème de cacao rather than dark and adds Champagne for a more balanced formula.

1 oz. Pierre Ferrand 1840 Cognac
½ oz. Lillet Blanc (or Cocchi Americano)
½ oz. Marie Brizard white crème de cacao
Champagne or other dry sparkling wine

Combine all ingredients but Champagne in your cocktail shaker, add ice, and shake for 15 seconds until well diluted. Double strain into a chilled coupe, top with bubbly.

Sidecar

The most famous classic cocktail featuring Cognac is a drier riff on the *Brandy Crusta* of the 19th century. Created in 1948, the *Sidecar* has evolved, mainly as different ingredients come in and out of vogue.

1½ oz. Pierre Ferrand Ambre Cognac
1 oz. Pierre Ferrand dry orange curaçao
¾ oz. lemon juice
1 tsp. simple syrup
Garnish: orange twist
Garnish: sugar rim (optional)

Prepare sugar rim on chilled coupe by rubbing cut lemon along rim and rolling in sugar (optional). Combine all the ingredients in a shaker with ice. Shake until chilled. Double strain into a chilled coupe. Express oils from orange twist over top of drink, notch on edge of rim.

Spiced Pear Old-Fashioned

I've used St. George Spirits products elsewhere in this book, and their spiced pear liqueur is the perfect Fall-to-Winter addition to your bar. This is an Old-fashioned variant[82] that ups the pear factor with my homemade pear syrup. Here you can also practice your flamed twist technique!

2 oz. bourbon whiskey
¾ oz. St. George spiced pear liqueur
1 tsp. pear syrup (page 70)
4 dashes Angostura bitters
Garnish: flamed orange twist

Combine all ingredients in shaker. Add ice and shake 10-15 seconds, double strain over a big rock in a chilled old-fashioned glass. Flame twist over glass, drop in.

Improved Chartreuse Swizzle

The "swizzle" is a whole class of cocktails named after the stick of the same name. The original swizzle sticks were created in the 18th century at a rum plantation in the West Indies using the branch of the *Quararibea Turbinata* (also known as the "swizzle stick tree").[83] This recipe is a fine example of the genre. Found on the KaiserPenguin.com website (is there a better drink blog name than that?), the formula is amped up by including so-called "jet fuel," aka overproof Jamaican rum.[84]

1½ oz. green Chartreuse
¼ oz. J. Wray & Nephew overproof rum
¾ oz. lime juice
1 oz. pineapple juice
½ oz. John D. Taylor velvet falernum
Garnish: 1 sprig mint & nutmeg

Combine all ingredients in shaker and add a half-handful of crushed ice. Whip shake well for 10-15 seconds or until ice is mostly dissolved, then strain over crushed ice in a 16 oz. pilsner. Top with more ice, garnish with lightly-slapped mint and an abundance of grated nutmeg. Serve with a straw nestled beside that fragrant mint.

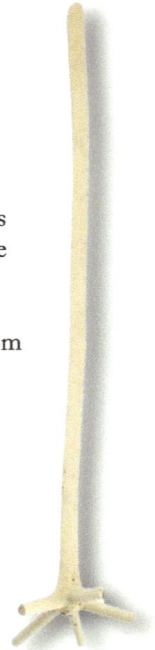

PINEAPPLE JUICE
Simply skin, core, and cut up a pineapple. Don't worry about getting every last eye or bit of core; throw into your food processor and strain to extract juice. Alternate: cold-pressed juice from the market. *Dole* cans - less ideal.

Billy the Oysterman No. 2

Growing up in historic Savannah, Georgia, our house served double duty as the home to my mom's rare book and print business called *The Printed Page*. Her books instilled in me a life-long love of reading. Getting into mixology during quarantine, I picked up several cocktail histories - I recommend anything written by David Wondrich - and spent a fair amount of time hunting down historic recipes online. This is one of those recipes from a 1934 booklet[85] by Lairds Distillery of New Jersey, the oldest in America and the recipient of Distillery License No. 1 from the U.S. Treasury in 1780.[86] This drink is named after a defunct New York City restaurant and its namesake cocktail.

Ingredients

1½ oz. Lairds Applejack
½ oz. Ransom Barrel-Aged Old Tom gin
½ oz. lemon juice
¼ oz. grenadine
¼ oz. Dolin Dry vermouth
Garnish: lemon twist

Directions

Add all ingredients to shaker. Add ice and shake for about 15 seconds. Double strain into a chilled coupe. Garnish with expressed lemon. Drop in or discard.

The Apple Bee

This is one of several holiday-themed original/adapted drinks I've created over the last 18 months. On Rosh Hashanah, the Jewish New Year, we traditionally enjoy apples and honey with a prayer for a sweet new year. I created the *Apple Bee* by drawing on a cocktail known as the *Golden Delicious*.[87] I've made this a little less boozy by increasing the apple flavor profile with muddled apples, and creating a smoother taste by swapping out higher-proof applejack with apple brandy. My first iteration of the drink, using Barenjager honey liqueur, tasted artificial. Honey-sweetened Bénédictine provides a more nuanced and herbal profile and makes for a much better drink.

Ingredients

2 oz. Clear Creek Reserve 8-year apple brandy
¾ oz. lemon juice
¾ oz. Bénédictine
¼ oz. honey syrup (3 parts honey to 1 part water)
¼ Honeycrisp or similar apple
Garnish: fan of thin apple slices

Directions

Roughly chop the apple and place in the bottom of shaking tin. Muddle apple well to release juices. Add remaining ingredients to tin, add ice and shake until well chilled, about 15 seconds. Double strain over a large rock in a double old-fashioned glass and garnish. *Shana Tovah!*

WHIP IT GOOD

The most prolonged, hardest shake is for drinks served up, like a daiquiri, while a rocks drink benefits from a shorter shake. The shake is faster still for drinks that will receive a "lengthener"—such as Champagne. The shortest shake of all is for a drink served over crushed ice. Called a "whip shake," an ounce or so of crushed ice is shaken until dissolved, chilling with minimal dilution.

Chapter Six:
The Sweet Stuff

These recipes are indeed a home bartender's best friend. None are terribly time-consuming, and there's really not much to mess up. If you can boil water, you can make these. But know this - the Roses lime and grenadine you may have bought in the past bear little resemblance to the real thing. No cocktail in this volume that calls for syrup is going to shine with those mass-produced versions. You can find higher quality commercial suppliers, and companies like Small Hand Foods and Liber are great go-to's for shelf-stable (until opened) alternatives. See *Resources* on page 72 for supplies and equipment.

Simple Syrup

1 part sugar
1 part water

My recipes calling for "simple syrup" refer to a 1:1 dilution. Rich simple syrup is 2:1 ratio, using two parts sugar to one part water. Rich syrup also has a longer shelf life.

Combine ingredients in a pot and heat gently until sugar dissolves. Do not boil. Allow to cool, then bottle. You can also vary the sugar type - demerara, raw cane, or brown. 1:1 syrup needs to be refrigerated and will last for a few weeks.

COPPER & METAL

The copper mug is the "required" vessel for serving mule cocktails - those that include a spirit, lime, and ginger beer. Why? Some say the inventor of the Moscow Mule in the 1940s bought a surplus of copper mugs off a friend. Regardless, copper is a great conductor that keeps the drink ice-cold.

Grenadine

Did you know grenadine is actually pomegranate syrup with a few other elements added for flavor? It's truly a far cry from Roses grenadine. Enjoy!

16 oz. POM 100% pomegranate juice
16 oz. raw sugar
2 oz. pomegranate molasses
1 tsp. orange blossom water

Heat juice slightly until it gets warm enough to dissolve sugar. Remove from heat. Add sugar, molasses, orange blossom water, and whisk gently. Allow to cool and then bottle. Lasts up to one month in the refrigerator.

Ginger Syrup

250 grams ginger root
250 grams white sugar
240 ml (1 cup) water

Measure by weight, not volume, for this recipe. Put ginger and sugar in blender or food processor and add boiling water. Blend thoroughly, then strain through a fine-mesh sieve. Bottle and store in fridge for up to a few weeks. Adding an ounce of high-proof vodka at the end of the process will increase longevity.

Penicillin Cocktail
2 oz. blended scotch
¾ oz. lemon juice
½ oz. ginger syrup
½ oz. honey syrup (diluted 1:1 with water)
¼ ounce Islay single malt scotch
Garnish: candied ginger & lemon twist

Another Sam Ross cocktail. Combine all in shaker, add ice and shake. Serve over fresh ice and garnish.

Lime Cordial

250 grams sugar (by weight)
8 oz./240 ml hot water (by volume)
1½ oz./45 ml lime juice (by volume)
1½ oz./45 ml grated lime peel (by volume)
1 oz./30 ml citric acid (measured by volume)

Combine all of the ingredients in a food processor or blender. Blend on medium speed for 30 seconds.[88] Strain with a fine strainer. Bottle and refrigerate. Note: food-grade citric acid sources can be purchased on Amazon. See Resources, page 72.

Gin Gimlet
2 oz. London dry gin
1 oz. lime cordial

Shake with ice until chilled and diluted, 15-30 seconds. Strain into a chilled coupe.

Oleo Saccharum

Quite literally, this is Latin for "sugared oil." Use this to sub for fresh juice + simple syrup.

Peel of 4 lemons or limes (no pith)
½ cup reserved lemon/lime juice
8 oz. sugar

Peel lemons. In a non-reactive bowl (e.g. stainless steel), muddle sugar and peel until sugar is well moistened. Cover and let sit for a few hours or up to a day, shaking occasionally. This will yield around 1 cup of syrup infused with your citrus. Strain, press on solids, and add to a small saucepan with 1 cup fresh water and ½ cup of freshly squeezed juice. Barely heat enough to dissolve any visible sugar. Strain and store in fridge.

Gomme Syrup

Gomme or gum syrup is simple syrup with the addition of gum acacia. You'll find food-quality gum acacia on Amazon (see page 72). It creates a fantastic mouthfeel and transforms your Old-fashioned into something extraordinary. For the best results, measure carefully.

2 oz. / 55 g gum arabic (gum acacia)
6 oz. / 180 ml water
12 oz. / 340 g superfine sugar

Amounts are critical here, so measure carefully. In a small plastic container, combine gum arabic and 2 oz. / 60 ml of the water. Stir with a chopstick to blend, add cover, and then leave at room temperature for 48 hours, or until the gum arabic is wholly absorbed by the water.

In a small pan, combine sugar and remaining water, heating gently until sugar begins to dissolve. Add in gum arabic mixture and stir. Immediately remove from heat and allow to cool, then bottle. Store in the fridge indefinitely.[89]

Orgeat Syrup

This is an almond syrup essential to many classic and tiki cocktail recipes.

2 cups plain unsweetened almond milk
4 cups granulated sugar
2 tbsp. almond extract
1 tsp. orange flower water
⅓ cup Cognac or overproof rum

In a medium saucepan, heat almond milk and sugar over medium-high, stirring until sugar is dissolved, 3-5 minutes. Remove from heat, stir in almond extract, orange flower water, and Cognac/rum. Cool and transfer to bottle and keep refrigerated. Will last 3-4 weeks.

Berry Syrup

This recipe works with any type of fresh berry.

2 cups fresh berries
1 cup water
1 cup sugar

In a small saucepan, simmer 2 cups fruit with 8 oz. water and 1 cup of sugar until the color has leached into the syrup, 5-10 minutes. Allow to cool. Add 1 oz. vodka, fine strain, and bottle.

Grapefruit Syrup

Save the candied peels for garnish.

½ cup grapefruit juice
½ cup sugar
½ tsp. grapefruit zest
¼ tsp. citric acid

In a small bowl, whisk the grapefruit juice with the sugar, zest, and citric acid until the sugar dissolves. Cover with plastic wrap, and refrigerate for at least 8 hours. Pour the syrup through a fine sieve into a bottle and store in the refrigerator.

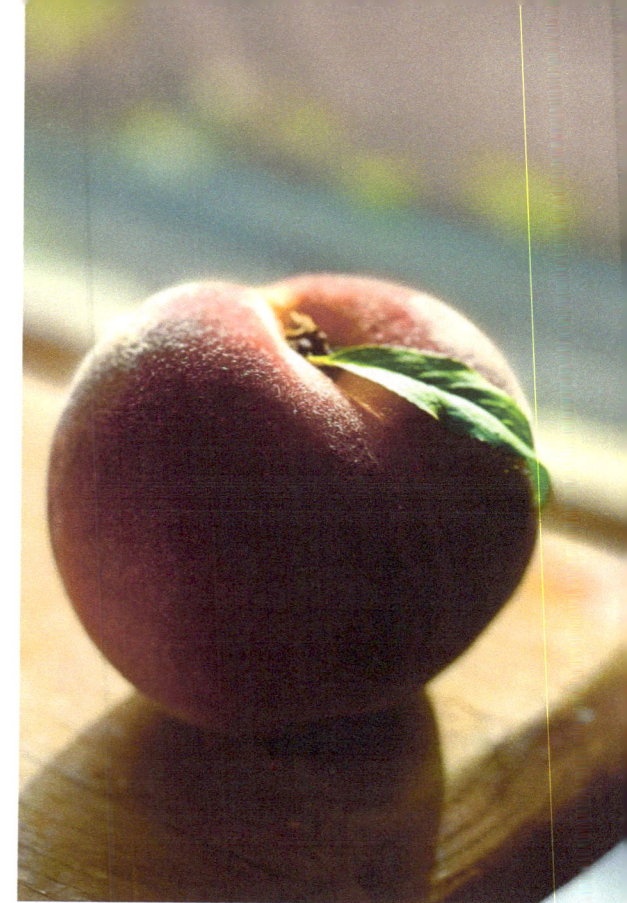

Pear & Stone Fruit

When pears and peaches are in plentiful supply, I've often made a syrup to capture their essence for my cocktail experiments.

8 oz. stone fruit (peach, pear, etc.)
16 oz. sugar
8 oz. water

Wash fruit well. Peel (optional), then coarsely chop. Combine with sugar and water in small saucepan and gently heat for 30 minutes to leach flavor from fruit. Do not allow to boil. Allow to cool, strain, then bottle.

Pineapple Syrup & The Ticonderoga Cup

One of my favorite restaurants here in Atlanta is a little place called the *Ticonderoga Club*. Founded by Regan Smith and Greg Best, they spearheaded Atlanta's cocktail renaissance in 2014, running the bar at *Holeman & Finch*. This take on the julep at *Ticonderoa* is their namesake drink and features pineapple syrup, sherry, and aged rum.[90] This is definitely among my top ten drinks of all time.

Ticonderoga Cup
1½ oz. English-style rum
1 oz. Cognac
½ oz. oloroso sherry
½ oz. lemon juice
½ ounce golden pineapple syrup (see below:)
Garnish: "a forest" of mint sprigs

Build in a shaker tin over ice. Shake and serve in a mug of your choice. Garnish with a forest of mint.

Pineapple Syrup
1 ripe pineapple
2 cups cane sugar
2 cups white sugar
4 cups water

Peel and core pineapple and cut into 1-inch cubes. Combine pineapple, sugars, and water in a saucepan, place over low heat, and stir. Simmer for 20 minutes. Once mixture has reached a simmer, and all sugar is broken down, increase heat to medium, stir well, and set a timer for one hour. Check occasionally and stir. Do not allow mixture to boil. Once the volume is reduced by half, remove from heat and allow to cool for about 15 minutes. Set a wire strainer over a large container and pour through the strainer. Press all of the liquid from the pineapple. Once all of the liquid has been pressed, refrigerate the sugared pineapple for other uses (over ice cream!) or discard. Strain the syrup again. Will last three weeks in refrigerator.

Resources

Like everything else, Amazon is a convenient source for many of the items you may want for your bartending arsenal. These are some products I can personally recommend:

- Novart XXL Glass Herb Keeper - keeps herbs fresh
- Epare Ice Cube Mold - for 2-inch crystal-clear ice cubes
- Pure Ingredients Gum Arabic - for gomme syrup, pg. 70
- Millard Citric Acid - for lime cordial, pg. 69
- Small Hand Foods syrups - pineapple gomme, orgeat
- Liber Syrups - a wide variety of small-batch syrups
- Lewis Bag & Hammer for perfectly snowy crushed ice
- Top Shelf Bar Supply heavy-duty silicone mat
- Estillo Easy Cap 8.5 oz. square bottles (for fridge-door storage)
- Jillmo Travel Bartender Bag
- Repour Wine Savers - reduces oxidation in opened wine
- Luxardo & Amarena cherries
- Fee Brothers - from my wife's hometown (Rochester, NY), a 5th-generation producer of bitters & syrups

Here are some directly-from-the-manufacturer sources:
- Cocktail & Sons - Fassionola Syrup, produced in a limited run each Spring (see Ferrel's Hurricane, pg. 42)
- Cocktail Kingdom - for most bar tools (some available on Amazon as well)
- Goodwill - cheap glassware. Yes, they won't match, but that's called "charming!"
- Target - Houdini pebble ice trays
- Crew Supply Company - maker of the "Chubby Bottle," ideal for storing your syrups or infusions, with a removable bottom for easy cleaning.

I encourage anyone wanting to learn more about this topic to check out any of the books I reference below and the citations I've noted to give credit where credit is due. I have to thank these authors for inspiring me to create this volume that relies heavily on their insights.

- *Cocktail Codex* by Alex Day, Nick Fuachald, David Kaplan, and Devon Tarby
- *Liquid Intelligence* by Dave Arnold
- *The Bar Book* by Jeffrey Morgenthaler
- *Smuggler's Cove* by Martin and Rebecca Cate
- *Regarding Cocktails* by Sasha and Georgette Petraske
- *Imbibe!* by David Wondrich
- *Meehan's Bartender Manual* by Jim Meehan

Here are some helpful websites, apps, and other digital tools:

- Mixel - iOS & Android - my most frequently used mixology reference. There is a free version, and it includes a wide variety of recipes. Their premium upgrade ($12) unlocks thousands more. Use the app to keep an inventory of all your spirits, garnishes, and what-not, and the best recommendations for what to make and buy next.
- Cocktail Party - web, iOS, and Android - another great mixology app that showcases drinks you can create from what you have on hand. Includes helpful commentary on each.
- KindredCocktails.com - comprehensive and dynamic site
- Liquor.com - great resource with extensive articles
- Cocktail Slut - cocktailvirgin.blogspot.com
- Difford's Guide - diffordsguide.com, an authoritative source
- Imbibe - imbibemagazine.com
- Punch - punchdrink.com
- Reddit - r/cocktails and r/mixology
- Lost Tiki Lounge - thelosttikilounge.com - source of big-batch cocktails and plenty of tiki mythology
- Kaiser Penguin - kaiserpenguin.com. Awesome tips, tricks and recipes
- AltonBrown.com - find Alton's epic eggnog recipe here

YouTube has many active mixology creators - these are my favorites:

- How To Drink
- Cocktail Chemistry
- Behind the Bar with Cara Devine
- The Educated Barfly
- Truffles on the Rocks
- Cocktails with Ciara
- Steve the Bartender
- Anders Erickson

And last but not least, my local liquor stores of choice:

- *My Friends Bottle Shop*, aka MFBS, is located close to my home in Grant Park, with friendly folks always willing to make recommendations and special orders
- *Elemental Spirits* - located in Poncey-Highland, another great store, offering plenty of eclectic choices and exclusive barrel picks

Cocktail Finder

*Denotes an original cocktail by the author

RYE WHISKEY

Rye has as many varieties as bourbon, but my go-to has become *Rittenhouse Bottled-in-Bond rye* ($25). At 100 proof, it has plenty of backbone to shine through and is delicious in a *Manhattan*, and pretty much anything else for that matter. *Sazerac Rye* ($24), originally distilled in New Orleans, is another inexpensive favorite that makes for the perfect *Sazerac*.

BOURBON

Bulleit ($26) is widely available, relatively inexpensive, pretty mellow, has just a trace of spice, and makes an excellent daily mixing bourbon. Although difficult to find in some areas, *Buffalo Trace* is smoother still ($30) and comes from the same distillery as the multi-thousand dollar bottles of *Pappy van Winkle* I dream of owning someday. My higher-end but fiscally responsible picks are *Widow Jane Straight Bourbon Whiskey 10 Yr* ($68) and *Old Forester 1920* 115-proof ($60).

COGNAC

Cognac is another must if you want to explore the cocktail classics. *Pierre Ferrand 1840* ($40) was created in conjunction with cocktail historian David Wondrich for the explicit purpose of mixed drinks. It comes in at 90-proof, not common in most modern VS Cognacs. *Pierre Ferrand Ambre* ($40) spends more time in oak and makes for the perfect *Sidecar*.

ORANGE LIQUEUR

Orange liqueurs find a home in dozens of cocktails in this book. *Pierre Ferrand Dry Orange Curaçao* ($30) is built off a Cognac-base, a common approach among orange liqueurs during the classic cocktail period. *Cointreau* ($30) and *Grand Marnier* ($30) are drier and sweeter options, respectively. If I had to pick one, the drier Pierre Ferrand is my first choice.

RUM

You'll want both a white rum and a dark. *Plantation 3-Stars* white rum ($20) is named for the three islands that comprise the blend. A funky Jamaican rum like *Smith & Cross Navy Strength* ($39) is the perfect complement. With a flavor that punches through even the fruitiest of tiki, it's fantastic. For something less aggressive, try *Plantation Original Dark* ($22). For a third type, a grassy unaged rhum agricole like *Clement Bleu* ($45) would be an ideal supplement to your collection and is a great way to experiment with split-base rum cocktails.

GIN

Gins range from very traditional to innovative styles from Japan, Germany, and the U.S., but you'll cover your needs well with a London dry. *Beefeater* is inexpensive and deliciously juniper-forward ($17). *Plymouth* ($34) is a softer and slightly sweeter gin that goes well in a wide variety of drinks. Its somewhat more viscous texture makes for a terrific martini. My favorite new-style gin is *Junipero* ($40) - it's a juniper flavor bomb!

Bottle Bar

SWEET VERMOUTH

Sweet vermouth, often simply referred to as red vermouth, is a critical cocktail component. I recommend the vanilla-forward *Carpano Antica* (375ml, $18) from Italy. For another flavor profile with more herbal notes, try *Cocchi di Torino* (750ml, $20). I try to buy vermouth in smaller bottles as they will only last for a few months once opened and stored in the fridge.

DRY VERMOUTH

Dolin Dry (375ml, $15) from France is a good bet, leaning towards citrus, with an absinthe/anise edge. *Noilly Pratt Extra Dry* (375ml, $10) is another French option that is drier still. Although transparent like dry vermouth, *Dolin Blanc* (375 ml, $10) is a relatively sweet option I use in many of my favorite recipes. *Cocchi Americano* (375ml, $15) is another good Italian option closer to *Dolin Blanc*. Like sweet vermouth, refrigerate these and toss after about one to two months after opening.

AGAVE

As a category, agave-based spirits have exploded over the last several years. You can spend a fortune on tequila, so save your *Clase Azul Reposado* ($175) for sipping neat. For mixing, you will want a blanco tequila, and my current favorite is *Fortaleza* ($55) that brings earthy, vegetal, and even savory notes to the party. For a slightly aged version, try *La Gritona Reposado* ($36). I'm not a massive fan of mezcal's signature smoky profile, but *Del Maguey VIDA* ($36) is an excellent value and ideal for mixing.

CLASSIC LIQUEURS

Green Chartreuse ($60) is an absolute necessity in many classic cocktails. *Luxardo Maraschino* cherry liqueur ($35) comes in a distinctive straw-wrapped bottle and fits in with everything from a *Daiquiri* to an *Old-fashioned*. If you're a fan of the *Aviation* or other floral flavors, pick up a bottle of *Rothman & Winter Creme de Violette* ($30).

AMARO & APERTIVO

A bottle of *Campari* ($30) will be the most useful for your basic amaro needs. My tastes tend toward *Aperol* ($20) for a slightly sweeter option. I would be remiss if I didn't mention my favorite in this category, *Amaro Nonino Quintessentia* ($50), a grappa-based, citrusy, bittersweet amaro enjoyable mixed or on the rocks. *Amaro Montenegro* ($40) is more widely available and subs well for *Nonino*. Either of these works in the modern classic, the *Paper Plane* cocktail, page 17.

BITTERS

If you only have room (or spousal approval) for a total of twelve bottles, there's one absolute necessity in the bitters category. The classic *Angostura* (5 oz., $10) adds a signature punch in numerous cocktails, while *Regan's Orange Bitters* (5 oz., $10) is a softer flavor perfect in a martini. If you enjoy anise/herbal flavors, try *Peychaud's Bitters* (5 oz., $8) from New Orleans. To add the baking-spice flavors needed in many tiki drinks, try *Bittermens' Elemakule* (5 oz., $15) or *Bittercube Jamaican No. 1 or 2* (5 oz., $20).

Index

Citations

1   Carusillo, C. (2014, December 10). Myth busts: The enduring legacy of breast-shaped glassware. Eater. Retrieved October 26, 2021, from https://www.eater.com/2014/12/10/7339903/breast-Champagne-coupe-marie-antoinette.

2   Meehan, Jim. "Whisk(e)y." Meehan's Bartender MANUAL, Ten Speed, California, 2017, pp. 295–305.

3   Pickerell, D. (2018, September). The rise and fall of craft whiskey - distilled spirits. Distilled Spirits Council. Retrieved October 27, 2021, from https://www.distilledspirits.org/wp-content/uploads/2018/09/The-Rise-and-Fall-of-Craft-Whiskey.pdf.

4   Macy, Tom. "Barrel Maturation." Tom Macy Cocktails, www.tommacy.com/barrelmaturation.

5   Pangolindo. "Amaro Mood." Kindred Cocktails, 29 Sept. 2018, kindredcocktails.com/cocktail/amaro-mood.

6   Amberg, Banjo. "Algonquin Cocktail. ." Imbibe Magazine, Clyde Common, Portland OR, 26 Aug. 2020, imbibemagazine.com/recipe/algonquin-cocktail-recipe/.

7   DiMonriva, L. (2020, November 30). Can you improve my first original cocktail? the bloom county. YouTube. Retrieved October 13, 2021, from https://www.youtube.com/watch?v=Wpd8gCeGNT0.

8   Licor 43. (2020, November 3). Licor 43 - Our history. Licor 43 - Global. Retrieved October 13, 2021, from https://www.licor43.com/our-history/.

9   Morgenthaler, Jeffrey. "I Make the Best Amaretto Sour in the World." Jeffrey Morgenthaler, 9 Feb. 2012, jeffreymorgenthaler.com/i-make-the-best-amaretto-sour-in-the-world/.

10   Rector, Sylvia. "The Last Word Is a Drink with a Fascinating Detroit Story." Detroit Free Press, 21 Nov. 2014, www.freep.com/story/entertainment/dining/sylvia-rector/2014/11/21/last-word-cocktail-born-detroit/70021018/.

11   Erickson, Anders. "Two Drinks to Know - Final Ward vs Monte Cassino - YouTube." YouTube, 26 Mar. 2021, www.youtube.com/watch?v=NGPSk_jMZvA.

12   Roennfeldt, Steven. "Final Ward Cocktail - a Last WORD RIFF from Death & Co, Nyc." Steve the Bartender, 10 Dec. 2020, stevethebartender.com.au/final-ward-cocktail-recipe-last-word-riff/.

13   Liquor.com. (2013, April 17). Bénédictine. Liquor.com. Retrieved October 27, 2021, from https://www.liquor.com/brands/benedictine/.

14   Liquor.com. (2020, November 19). The ultimate bourbon drink you've never heard of. Liquor.com. Retrieved October 24, 2021, from https://www.liquor.com/recipes/the-paper-plane/.

15   Madrusan, Michael. "Apertif Hour." Spot at the Bar: Welcome to the Everleigh, Hardie Grant Books, 2017.

16   Fonseca, Gabe, and Polite Provisions, San Diego. "Surf Liner Rye Whiskey Cocktail." Imbibe Magazine, 26 Aug. 2020, imbibemagazine.com/recipe/surf-liner/.

17   Cocktail Party. (2019, August 19). Dale's julep. Cocktail Party. Retrieved October 13, 2021, from https://cocktailpartyapp.com/drinks/dales-julep/.

18   "'The king then removed his signet ring from his hand and gave it to Haman the son of Hamdasa the Agagi, the oppressor of the Jews." The Book of Esther 3:10.

19   Petraske, Sasha, and Georgette Moger-Petraske. "Cosmonaut." Regarding Cocktails, Phaidon Press Limited, London, 2017, pp. 92–93.

20   Meehan, Jim, et al. "Gin and Genever." Meehan's Bartender Manual, Ten Speed, California, 2017, pp. 203–213.

21   Eva, R. (2018, April 19). The clover club cocktail - history, recipe, Technique & Variations. Standard Spoon. Retrieved October 21, 2021, from https://www.standardspoon.com/blogs/the-cocktail-ritual/the-clover-club-cocktail-history-recipe-technique-variations-1.

22   Reiner, Julie. "Clover Club Cocktail." Imbibe Magazine, 31 Mar. 2020, imbibemagazine.com/recipe/clover-club/.

23   Gray, K. (2020, November 22). Corpse reviver no. 2. Liquor.com. Retrieved October 25, 2021, from https://www.liquor.com/recipes/corpse-reviver-no-2/.

24   "Corpse Reviver No. 2." Savoy Cocktail Book, Constable, London, 1930.

25   "Absinthe." Wikipedia, Wikimedia Foundation, 7 Sept. 2021, en.wikipedia.org/wiki/Absinthe.

26   Roennfeldt, Steven. "Sunflower Cocktail Recipe - a Corpse Reviver No. 2 VARIATION!" Steve the Bartender, 10 Dec. 2020, stevethebartender.com.au/sunflower-gin-elderflower-cocktail-recipe/.

27   Wondrich, David. "Behind the Drink: The French 75." Liquor.com, Liquor.com, 9 July 2012, www.liquor.com/articles/behind-the-drink-the-french-75/.

28   Judge. (n.d.). 1927 here's how by judge Jr (2nd impression). Page 28. Retrieved October 25, 2021, from https://euvs-vintage-cocktail-books.cld.bz/1927-Here-s-

How-2nd-impression/28.

29   "French 75" Savoy Cocktail Book, Constable, London, 1930.

30   Day, Alex, et al. "High Five." Cocktail Codex: Fundamentals, Formulas, Evolutions, Ten Speed Press, California, 2018, p. 133.

31   Teague, Sother. "Waterproof Watch." Imbibe Magazine, Amor Y Amargo , Brooklyn, 11 Sept. 2020, imbibemagazine.com/recipe/amor-amargo-waterproof-watch/.

32   Adapted from Death & Co.; and Phil Ward. "Elder Fashion Recipe." Chowhound, 19 Apr. 2017, www.chowhound.com/recipes/elder-fashion-11154.

33   Meehan, Jim, and Chris Gall. "Cherry Pop Cocktail." The Pdt Cocktail Book: The Complete Bartender's Guide from the Celebrated Speakeasy, Sterling, New York, 2012.

34   Bradsell, Dick, and Punch Magazine. "Bramble." PUNCH, 13 Jan. 2021, punchdrink.com/recipes/bramble/.

35   Ward, Phil, and Death & Co. "Celine Fizz." Cocktail Party, 30 June 2020, cocktailpartyapp.com/drinks/celine-fizz/.

36   DiMonriva, Leandro. "Ramos Gin Fizz Redux - YouTube." YouTube, 21 Jan. 2021, www.youtube.com/watch?v=rMRf3858Yrg.

37   "Friulians." Minority Rights Group, Minority Rights Group International, 19 Nov. 2020, minorityrights.org/minorities/friulians/. Also: Elliot, Justin, et al. "Friûl Libar." Kindred Cocktails, 4 Jan. 2017, kindredcocktails.com/cocktail/friul-libar.

38   "Negroni." Spirits Beacon, spiritsbeacon.com/cocktails/recipes/negroni-1.

39   Roennfeldt, Steven. "Unusual Negroni Cocktail Recipe - Gin, Aperol AND Lillet Blanc." Steve the Bartender, 10 Dec. 2020, stevethebartender.com.au/unusual-aperol-negroni-cocktail-recipe/.

40   Traverse, Maxence. "Negroni NONINO." Negroni Nonino - Grappa Nonino, 2011, www.grappanonino.it/en/aperitifs-and-cocktails/negronino.

41   Dixon, Beth, and Pasture, Richmond VA. "Bermuda Hundred." Saveur, 15 July 2015, www.saveur.com/gin-pineapple-campari-cocktail-recipe/.

42   Meehan, J. (2017). Spirits & Cocktails: Rum and Cachaca. In Meehans Bartender Manual - A Cocktail Handbook for hosts (pp. 238–245). essay, Ten Speed Press.

43   Cate, M., & Cate, R. (2016). Smuggler's cove: Exotic cocktails, rum, & the cult of tiki. Ten Speed Press.

44   Petraske, Sasha, and Georgette Moger-Petraske. "Daiquiri" Regarding Cocktails, Phaidon Press Limited, London, 2017, pp. 94-95.

45   Cate, Martin, and Rebecca Cate. "The Birth of Tiki: Aku Aku." Smuggler's Cove: Exotic Cocktails, Rum and the Cult of Tiki, Ten Speed Press, New York, 2016, p. 39.

46   Difford, Simon. "French Daiquiri Cocktail Recipe." Cocktail Recipe, 4 Aug. 2016, www.diffordsguide.com/cocktails/recipe/793/french-daiquiri.

47   Boudreau, Jamie. "Stiggins Daiquiri No. 2." The Canon Cocktail Book: Recipes from the Award-Winning Bar, Houghton Mifflin Harcourt, Boston, 2016, p. 88.

48   Nast, Condé. "Hemingway Daiquiri." Epicurious, Epicurious, 24 Jan. 2012, www.epicurious.com/recipes/food/views/hemingway-daiquiri-390814.

49   Cate, Martin, and Rebecca Cate. "Rum Through the Ages." Smuggler's Cove: Exotic Cocktails, Rum and the Cult of Tiki, Ten Speed Press, New York, 2016, p. 144

50   Cate, Martin, and Rebecca Cate. "Rum Through the Ages." Smuggler's Cove: Exotic Cocktails, Rum and the Cult of Tiki, Ten Speed Press, New York, 2016, p. 150

51   Adams, Jenny. "Reclaiming the Hurricane." Garden & Gun, 6 June 2016, gardenandgun.com/recipe/reclaiming-the-hurricane/.

52   Slabiak, Selma. "Freydis." Spirit of the North: Cocktail Recipes and Stories from Scandinavia, TeNeues Publishing Group, Kempen, Germany, 2018.

53   Punch, et al. "Recipe: Easy Tiki: Artichoke Hold." PUNCH, 30 Nov. 2020, punchdrink.com/recipes/artichoke-hold/.

54   "Big Batch Tiki Cocktails: Step-by-Step Guide Recipes, Tips & Tricks." The Lost Tiki Lounge, 15 Oct. 2020, thelosttikilounge.com/cocktails/big-batch-guide/.

55   Yarm, Frederic. "Bikini Atoll." Cocktail Virgin Slut, 13 Oct. 2011, http://cocktailvirgin.blogspot.com/2011/10/bikini-atoll.html.

56   Day, Alex, et al. "The Sidecar." Cocktail Codex: Fundamentals, Formulas, Evolutions, Ten Speed Press, California, 2018, p. 168.

57   Lebovitz, D. (2020, June 1). El Presidente Cocktail. David Lebovitz. Retrieved October 22, 2021, from https://www.davidlebovitz.com/el-presidente-cocktail-julio-cabrera-recipe-vermouth-rum-triple-sec/.

58   Pearson, Zachary. "Honeymusk." Kindred Cocktails, 22 Apr. 2011, kindredcocktails.com/cocktail/honeymusk.

59   Magyarics, K. (2021, January 16). Funky rum: Everything you need to know about the booming trend. Liquor.com. Retrieved October 22, 2021, from https://www.liquor.com/articles/hogo-rum/.

60   Brown, Alton. "Aged Eggnog Recipe." Alton Brown, 16 Nov. 2020, altonbrown.com/recipes/aged-eggnog/.

61   Morgenthaler, Jeffrey. "Egg Nog (Base Recipe)." Jeffrey Morgenthaler, 10 Nov. 2009, jeffreymorgenthaler.com/egg-nog/.

62   Cate, Martin, and Rebecca Cate. "Curating the Experience." Smuggler's Cove: Exotic Cocktails, Rum and the Cult of Tiki, Ten Speed Press, New York, 2016, p. 134.

63   "Grog - Etymology." Wikipedia, Wikimedia Foundation, 29 Sept. 2021, en.wikipedia.org/wiki/Grog.

64   Cate, Martin, and Rebecca Cate. "Three Dots and a Dash." Epicurious, Epicurious, 18 May 2016, www.epicurious.com/recipes/food/views/three-dots-and-a-dash.

65   Meehan, Jim, et al. "Tequila and Mezcal." Meehan's Bartender Manual, Ten Speed, California, 2017, pp. 269–279.

66   Arnold, D., & Huggett, T. (2014). Salt. In Liquid intelligence: The art and science of the perfect cocktail (p. 61). essay, W.W. Norton & Company, Inc.

67   Kaplan, David, et al. "The Specs: Agave, Shaken." Death & Co: Modern Classic Cocktails, with More than 500 Recipes, Ten Speed Press, Berkeley, 2014, p. 189.

68   Day, Alex, et al. "Appendix." Cocktail Codex: Fundamentals, Formulas, Evolutions, Ten Speed Press, California, 2018, p. 282.

69   Kirkland Tap & Trotter, Somerville, MA. "Santa Rosa." Kindred Cocktails, 7 Nov. 2013, kindredcocktails.com/cocktail/santa-rosa.

70   Punch. "Oaxaca Old-Fashioned." PUNCH, 13 Jan. 2021, punchdrink.com/recipes/oaxaca-old-fashioned/.

71   "Cantarito." Cocktail Party, 17 Apr. 2020, cocktailpartyapp.com/drinks/cantarito/.

72   "Dos Besitos." Cocktail Party, 30 Jan. 2020, cocktailpartyapp.com/drinks/dos-besitos/.

73   Dean, Lily, and Old Kentucky Bourbon Bar, Covington, KY. "Avion De Papel." Kindred Cocktails, 17 Aug. 2017, kindredcocktails.com/cocktail/avion-de-papel.

74   Courvoisier. "Cognac History & Origin: Courvoisier®." Courvoisier, 1 Jan. 1970, https://www.courvoisier.com/us/history/.

75   Meehan, Jim, et al. "Brandy and Eau De Vie." Meehan's Bartender MANUAL, Ten Speed, California, 2017, pp. 343–350.

76   Weigand, Alex, and Bambara, Cambridge, Massachusetts. "Lady Amaro, a GIN COCKTAIL." Imbibe Magazine, 17 Mar. 2020, imbibemagazine.com/recipe/lady-gin-cocktail/.

77   Petraske, Sasha, and Georgette Moger-Petraske. "The Sour, Champs-Elysees." Regarding Cocktails, Phaidon Press Limited, London, 2017, pp. 90–91.

78   Febles, Rafa Garcia. "Y Control." Kindred Cocktails, 2014, kindredcocktails.com/cocktail/y-control.

79   Liquor.com. (2020, November 8). A good sazerac is like Boozy Yin-yang. Liquor.com. Retrieved October 17, 2021, from https://www.liquor.com/recipes/sazerac/.

80   No. 9 Park, Boston MA. "Fire in the Orchard." Kindred Cocktails, 21 Nov. 2013, kindredcocktails.com/cocktail/fire-in-the-orchard.

81   Lasher-Walker, T. (2019, October 22). An iron fist in a velvet glove; how the hand in glove was the result of a 'happy accident'. Tom Lasher Walker. Retrieved October 22, 2021, from https://tomlasherwalker.com/2019/10/21/an-iron-fist-in-a-velvet-glove-how-the-hand-in-glove-was-the-result-of-a-happy-accident/.

82   St. George Spirits. "Spiced Pear Old-Fashioned." St. George Spirits :: Cocktails Featuring Spiced Pear Liqueur, www.stgeorgespirits.com/cocktails-featuring/liqueurs/spiced-pear-liqueur/.

83   Fergus, J. "What's a Swizzle Stick and How Do You Use It? - the Manual." The Manual, The Manual, 6 Sept. 2017, www.themanual.com/food-and-drink/swizzle-stick/.

84-85   KP, Rick. "Improved Chartreuse SWIZZLE: Kaiser Penguin." Kaiser Penguin, 8 Nov. 2010, http://www.kaiserpenguin.com/improved-chartreuse-swizzle/.

86   Lairds Distillery. "1934 Lairds Applejack How to Serve Recipes." Lairds Applejack - How to Serve, Made with FlippingBook, 1934, euvs-vintage-cocktail-books.cld.bz/1934-Lairds-Applejack-How-To-Serve-Recipes/22.

87   Shelby Vittek | | January 27. "The Story behind Laird & Company, Our Country's Oldest Distillery." New Jersey Monthly, 28 Jan. 2021, njmonthly.com/articles/eat-drink/laird-and-company-oldest-distillery.

88   Food Dept. "Golden Delicious Cocktail Recipe from Rye House." Tasting Table, 15 Jan. 2010, www.tastingtable.com/cook/recipes/Golden-Delicious-Cocktail-Recipe-from-Rye-House.

89   Morgenthaler, Jeffrey. "How to Make Your Own Lime Cordial (Rose's Lime Juice)." Jeffrey Morgenthaler, 10 Aug. 2018, jeffreymorgenthaler.com/lime-cordial/.

90   Morgenthaler, J., Holmberg, M., Hale, A. (2014). Gum Syrup. In Bar Book: Elements of Cocktail Technique (p. 91). essay, Chronicle Books.

91   Greg, Best, and Punch. "Ticonderoga Cup." PUNCH, 6 May 2016, punchdrink.com/recipes/ticonderoga-cup/.

Acknowledgements

Thank you all so much for your support via Facebook, Instagram & IRL through the course of my cocktail journey.

Betsy Hill Armstrong
Greg Asman
Laurie Dean Baird
David & Ronni Beker
Jonathan Bellack
Jonathan Beltran
Brad Bender
Greg Best
Mary Bewig
Ben Barokas
Rob Beeler
Mindy Binderman
Leora Blumberg Rubinstein
Maria Breza
Midge Brown
Jeff Burkett
Kory Burke
Jonathan Carson
Marc Case
Melissa Chapman
David Cohen
Dennis Colon
Rina Cook
Ben Crain
Paul Donsky
Kelly Eberhardt & Paul Holbrook
Jay & Susan Eldridge
Dawn Epstein Berlinsky
Jonathan Ernst
Jeremy Fain
Amanda Forgione
Lucy Fry
Teri Gallo

Jim Gerberich
Danny Glusman
Steven Gold
Andrew & Holly Goldberg
Robert Granfeldt
Leon Gurevich
Dan Halioua
Allen Handelman & Barb Cote
Marty & Sherrie Handelman
Amy, Eric & Carter Handelman
Jeanne Handelman
Jon Harmer
Eric Heller
Dave Helmreich
Greg Herald
Debbie Herz-Huttner
Chris Hill
Jeremy Hlavacek
Eric Hochberg
Lisa, Jaimey, Dylann,
   Taylor & Kailey Hogan
Shane & Victoria Holland
Peter Horan
Sherilyn Hufford
Emily & Warren Hutmacher
Stacy & Skip Jennings
Scott Kent
Mike Kivort
Doug Lauretano
Josh Lawson
Mallory Lehn
Nancy Lucas
James Manring

Peyton Marcus
Aaron & Amanda Marks
Adina Marks
Scott Martin
Tina Maudsley
Rick McKee
Moira McKenna
Mike McLeod
Mitchell & Malcom McMillan
Betty Meltzer
David Meltzer
Scott Messer
Seth Miller
Matt Milligan
Eric Mischel
Bill Morrow
Louise Mulherin
Julia Muller
Hillel Norry
Robert Occhialini
Dena O'Neal
Matt O'Neill
Tony Orr
Rob Pickeral
Greg Pins & Benay Krissel
Eric Porres
Bob Rives
Steve Roach
Alanna Roazzi-Laforet
Ana & Eric Robbins
Tim Roche
Ken Rona & Ginger Fay
Tova Rose

Randall Rothenberg
Kristina Rudinskas
Lee Sachnoff
Julie, Scott, Austin & Mason Sagan
Jay & Kate Sandhaus
Nick Schingel
Brittany & Alan Schwartzwald
Jana & John Seven
Jeremy & Marissa Shedrow
Jamie Sieder
Bobby Siegel
Joel, Rachel, Sophie & Mira Silverman
Adam Silverman
Rande Anmuth Simpson
Eric Smith
Regan Smith
Robert Smyth
Laurel Snyder & Chris Poma
Casey Steele
Karen Sterman
Andrea Su
Lori Tavoularis
Kari Traud
Seth Trotz & Cynthia Meyersburg
Kara Weber
Ron Weber
Jaime Wender
Jason White
Jarred Wilichinsky
Susan Fellman-Witkowski
Steve Wohl
Jonathan Young & Lonna Pack
Terri Zuckerman

**Without the support of friends far and near,
I might never have discovered my favorite drinks here.**